Perfect Partners?

Love, sex, marriage and friendship

Bob Mullan

TVS

For Garry and Marie Carmen

First published in Great Britain in 1988
by Boxtree Limited.

Text copyright © 1988 Bob Mullan

ISBN 1 85283 209 6 (hbk)
ISBN 1 85283 214 2 (pbk)

Typeset by York House Typographic Limited
Printed and bound in Great Britain by
Richard Clay Ltd. London
for Boxtree Limited, 36 Tavistock Street,
London WC2E 7PB

Contents

Acknowledgements

I must firstly thank Sarah Mahaffy at Boxtree for her interest and under-standing, let alone endless patience. Peter Williams and Pippa Cross at TVS have also been supportive. Garry Marvin with his secretarial skills has been a great help, as has Eileen Urwin.

Finally I would like to thank Richard Denyer for supplying such apt photographs. Some of them are from his 'affinity and kindred' exhibition of studio portraits.

Front cover illustration Copyright: Chicpix

Other books by Bob Mullan

Stevenage Ltd
Approaching Social Theory with Ernest Cashmore
Life as Laughter: Following Bhagwan Shree Rajneesh
The Mating Trade
Uninvited Guests with Laurie Taylor
Sociologists on Sociology
The Enid Blyton Story
Zoo Culture with Garry Marvin
Are Mothers Really Necessary?

Preface

> 'I can't tell you why, he says one night to a friend. It's just every time I start on an affair, I know it's going to end. The end of everything is in the beginnings for me. It's going through the motions.'
>
> Norman Mailer *The Naked and the Dead*

It is difficult not to share the pessimism of Mailer's anti-war novel. Human, sexual and emotional relationships are invariably less than complete, often unsatisfactory and regularly disastrous. Yet we carry on. Like Mailer's Bob Hearn, who knows his first kiss is doomed, we too fantasise about our loved one, find her, love her and leave her. Or, more usually, we live a life of unfulfilled emotional promise. The average case of coupledom is a necessary but gruesome compromise; a diminution of our individual qualities, hopes and dreams. And for what? For tradition, respectability and the service of illusion. And once into a relationship it *is* hard to get out unscathed. The world map is dotted with the statistics of unrequited love, separation, divorce, extra-marital deceit, loneliness, resentment, bitterness, single-parents, emotionally deprived children and adults, crimes of passion and premature death. But, you will say, we know people whose individual lives have meshed into a meaningful, fruitful and rewarding togetherness. Through and with each other they have become better people. Well yes, such people *do* exist and are *lucky*. So we can hope. Indeed Mailer himself, writing about *The Naked and*

1

Dead, is interesting: 'The book finds man corrupted, confused to the point of helplessness, but it also finds that there are limits beyond which he cannot be pushed, and it finds that even in his corruption and sickness there are yearnings for a better world.'

My aim in this book is to discuss some of the issues raised by our search for perfect partners – no easy matter. For a start, knowledge, the faculty of reason, is only part of the equation. Luck, as I have suggested, plays a central role, as do *feelings* – our psychological states and predispositions which range from nervousness to impetuosity, rage, passion and madness. There are also questions of culture, of mores and of norms, of tradition. And there is the added fact that we are essentially in the dark as to what our 'partner' feels, thinks or does. However open and honest we all claim to be with each other, the reality is clouded. Ultimately we have solitary minds and bodies, and we do with them what we desire.

Consequently, whatever I may come up with will only take us so far. The matter of human relationships – what makes some last and what breaks others apart – is too deep and often murky an area of life to be analysed comprehensively. In any event, do we really want to know everything, even if it were possible? I don't hanker after more knowledge as I constantly live in the hope that something new, mysterious and ultimately meaningful will happen. My own life, uninteresting as it is, is a useful starting point, particularly as it will become clear what I am looking for.

I am not including material from my personal life as an exercise in self–indulgence, but for two reasons. To begin with, it seems clear to me that in matters of love, sex and relationships we are *all* of us expert witnesses. Although our own experiences are in a sense unique, on occasions they also follow familiar patterns. I believe we should judge the material written on the subject in terms of how it conforms to *our* experience. Secondly, there is the question of bias. The men and women who write on love often do not include themselves in their analyses. They tend to talk as if love somehow stops at their doorstep – seeming to refer to the world 'out there', of you and me, as if their lives were somehow different. If, for example, we were to read a book on the traumas of divorce, it would be useful to know of the author's experience of this, if any, which might explain its bias. I am not pointing fingers. Inevitably, our own personal experience, personal dilemmas and pain become woven into whatever we write. Indeed they are the source of fiction and much else besides, including what passes for 'objective' scholarship. I simply feel that this should be made clear so that we are able, so to speak, to read the book's subtext.

I once knew a clinical psychologist who believed in 'behaviour therapy'. This, for the uninitiated, is the psychological therapy which treats symptoms as if they were actually causes. In the treatment of spider phobia, for example, the patient might be sensitively encouraged to touch such a creature while listening to some soothing music. Little or no reference would be made to the possible origins of his fears. Similarly, in the case of male transvestism, a patient could well be given an electric shock at the sight of female clothing in an attempt to avert future cross-dressing behaviour. Again, the origins of his penchant would not be considered important. Anyway, my acquaintance regularly practised behaviour therapy – except when it came to his own daughter's psychological problems. For her, instead, it was the psychoanalytic couch and the slow but dramatic re-enactment of her childhood. This lesson has taught me to look extremely carefully at the relationships between people and the ideas they produce. I suppose it is simply another variation of the 'Karl Marx theorem': Marx analysed marriage as female domestic slavery, yet privately he wanted women to be his slaves. So now when I read that a marine biologist believes there is no conservation problem, I want to know if he eats fish. If you see what I mean.

I was the second-born child of two people who, like so many others, then and today, lived their lives *through* their children. They were honest, religious, exploited, working-class people. Having perhaps realised that they could achieve little more with their own lives, in their early thirties they decided on children. This is not surprising, of course; they had neither the opportunities, support, talents, aspirations nor luck to launch them on the merry-go-round of 'career' and career advancement. They knew, however, that any children they had would be *theirs*, and that no one could take *that* away from them. My early years were happy. I was loved, knew it and felt it. But as I grew older and as my parents' energy declined, I had a

3

sense of foreboding. I can vividly remember waiting for my mother to return home from work; I would wait in the dark, refusing to put the light on in case it would somehow spoil my feelings of being left, of feeling neglected, of waiting, and, naturally, reduce the joy I felt on her return. Philip Larkin writes of his own parents: 'They were rather awkward people and they were never very good at being happy. And these things rub off.' And so with my family, not just my parents but also my sister, I always felt a sense of doom, of disaster. They were never very demonstrative with each other, but my father *could* cry and my mother *could* hug. As an adolescent I sensed that they were living totally for their children, for us, and I always wished they wouldn't.

Just after retirement, my father died of cancer. A few days before his death I visited him in a depressing, under-staffed, poorly painted and dimly lit hospital ward. Partly through pain and anger, partly through pain-killing drugs, and partly through hindsight and perception, he said some unflattering things about my mother and their life together. I was shocked. They had always seemed 'as one', even if somewhat undemonstrative. It had appeared to me that his illness had brought them even closer. I was still shocked when, tearfully, we buried him. At the family gathering that followed I attempted to comfort my mother, suggesting that I could in some sense replace my father in her life – show her more of my love, give her less trouble. She told me that was impossible, that she had loved him *so* much, but then proceeded – as my father a week previously – to spell out their difficulties. A year later *she* died. Perhaps this is understandable. As death approaches, or as the pain of losing a loved one strikes home, possibly the anger at such a loss drives us to bitterness. Or is it perhaps a final act of clarity?

My parents' lives, like those of most ordinary, good and honest people, were grounded in survival, religious sentiment, goodwill to others, their children and Christmas. My own is very different. I am convinced that there has to be some ultimate purpose and meaning in life other than the urge to reproduce, yet I believe religion to be a pompous and ironic deceit. My goodwill towards others is extremely circumspect. I am not, as they were, steady in emotions. I am wildly ambitious; and in my personal life I have not been able, or prepared, to keep my disabilities from surfacing. I have been divorced twice,

4

have hurt people, including my own children, and have not really experienced the state of contentment.

Is my life so different to theirs because of my generation, the period in which I have lived? Is it due to a determination, or unconscious urge, not to repeat a pattern? Can it be attributed to the relationships I experienced in my early family life and their subsequent effect on my own relationships? Or is there no connection whatsoever? My argument is that we are *both* victims and beneficiaries of our times and our family histories, and that moreover we are not always a passive partner in these matters. Childhood is not without its purpose and promise; but history and *luck* also play their part. Again the work of Mailer is instructive. For in his novels, in common with some other writers, he searches for a means whereby he can portray the history of the particular man, the individual man, which both reflects *and* transforms the history of the social and cultural forces that surround him.

In this book I hope to throw some light on issues which I see both as important and personally inescapable. Life, however, is not all gloom and doom. On occasions it is emotionally gratifying, it can lift the spirit, and often it is very funny. So don't expect me to be serious all the time.

1

Why my pet monkey doesn't enjoy the New York Times

'"Do you like squid?" I asked, perusing the menu. Rule number three: "Pretend to be open to new experiences, beginning with gastronomical." "Each and every tentacle," he lied. The next time I saw Greg he'd read five more chapters of the *Pretend You're Sensitive* handbook and was able to ask me if I had an immediate family. Rule number four: "Notice she has parents, perhaps siblings. Ask about them." Midway through dinner I realized that he had studied the chapter on eye contact thoroughly; he could synchronize looking me in the eye and using my first name perfectly. The effect was devastating; I almost had to leave the table. Greg was pretending to be so sensitive that I almost thought he was.'

Jean Gonick

I acquired my pet monkey after reading the *Naked Ape*. I liked the levelling effect of Desmond Morris's book and despite my better judgement have since viewed animals anthropomorphically, imputing human emotions to them. At the zoo I 'see' monkeys cry and tigers rage; and I am always upset when I see those sad little penguins. Intellectually, I know it's nonsense. My pet monkey doesn't talk about me to his mates – in any case he has none now that he lives in a Victorian town house – and he certainly doesn't write

6

about me, unless he does so by candlelight when I'm asleep. Albert Camus, another great monkey lover, once remarked that when twentieth-century man is remembered it will be said that he 'fornicated, read the newspaper, and then the matter is exhausted'. Well, that's not the whole story. Twentieth-century man has begun to destroy the planet, its people and animals at an unprecedented pace. Furthermore, man's belief in his intellectual mastery has never been so illusory. Of course we have progressed with our inventions, have developed medical technologies, have solved some mathematical puzzles, have even put men on the moon; but we are no further forward in our understanding of the human condition, of the human spirit, or of the relationships we have with others which form the hub of our lives. Can we describe our emotions any better than did the poets of earlier centuries? Do we know why we love one person rather than another? Have we understood *precisely* the significance and meaning of sex in our lives? No. There are a number of reasons for this which I shall mention shortly.

After leaving school, and after numerous jobs – van driver, driller and machinist, bank clerk, hospital porter, labourer, and so on – I worked in a hospital with the mentally ill, read R.D. Laing and realised I wanted to know more about the human mind. I did not possess grandiose ambitions; I had no interest in becoming an expert on the exact functions of the hypothalamus, or the role of the pituitary in emotional and sexual behaviour, and I certainly did not want to know more about intelligence testing. Rather I wanted to know the answers to some general questions – why am I happy on some days and not others? Why doesn't anyone like me? Why do some people kill themselves? Why do some people end up in hospital believing they are Napoleon?

In due course I went to university, as a mature student, to read psychology, and as an added bonus enrolled for the philosophy courses. If I hoped to get all the answers, I was soon disillusioned. At my first seminar on ethics the professor turned to me and in all seriousness asked me 'what constitutes a *good* bacon sandwich?' Only later did I realise that this was one of the central questions of contemporary philosophy. Once I enquired innocently about courses on Sartre or Camus. 'They're not *real* philosophers,' came the guffawed reply. And one day I was so bold as to ask the professor the central existential question, 'Why am I here?' 'Because you passed your "A" levels,' was the mirthful reply.

I decided to abandon my sub-career in philosophy, despite the social benefits of calling yourself a philosopher – 'Oh he's deep you know' – when I was forced to read Wittgenstein. I surfaced from that particularly nasty encounter knowing simply that he had a penchant for deck chairs and carrier bags. I turned to sociology instead; well at least it talked about facts and figures, I reasoned. I could indeed handle sociology although the particular professor who taught me was a little on the simple side. When discussing Talcott Parsons and *functionalism*, he'd say things like, 'We all fit neatly together as parts of a system, don't we?'. 'What do you mean, Sir?' we'd reply. 'Well,' he'd begin his forty minute monologue, 'when I got on the train this morning a ticket collector collected my ticket, a porter carried my case, a taxi-driver brought me here, and I paid him. In other words, I fitted in with him as much as he fitted in with me. See what I mean?' Zzzzzzz.

Psychology was an even greater disappointment. I had forebodings, in fact, on day one. My tutor asked me endless questions about statistics, computation and my feeling about rodents. 'Rodents, sir?' 'Yes, rats. Albino-laboratory-reared-rats.' I soon discovered that academic psychology was centrally concerned with animals, not you and me. When it *was* concerned with you and me it was not at the emotional or sexual level. Rather it was at the level of 'selective attention' and other mundane mental processes. Things like the 'cocktail party problem', in other words the superhuman feat of listening or attending to one conversation when there's lots of noise around us. I used to study that. I spent most of my time sending rats down mazes or watching films of pigeons playing ping-pong. Soon I became disturbed at the cruelty to animals perpetrated in the name of science and decided I wanted no more of it. The more I read of experiments *designed* to create experimental neurosis in cats, of 'kitten carousels' where cats reared in complete darkness were then made to work a carousel in a striped drum to prove some obvious point about perception, the more I realised it was a decadent subject and not for me.

Events have moved on since my day. A 'distinguished' contemporary psychologist now nails cats' eyes to a board and spins the cats round, all in the name of progress.

The final straw came when I had a heart-to-heart with the professor of psychology. I was seeking reassurance and guidance, hoping that he could paint a rosier picture and urge me to stay. He suggested I write an essay, and he would accordingly assess my potential after reading it. 'Ok, on what?' He thought for a moment and then replied, 'Why not have a bash at the navigational skills of the goldfish?'. '*Goodbye*, Sir.' I transferred to sociology, but carried on reading psychology, concentrating on the individuals who dealt with the questions that most interested me.

With Freud I believe that much of our behaviour is unconsciously and irrationally motivated, a result of the psychological and sexual struggles going on since childhood. With B.F. Skinner I have to believe that some of our behaviour is shaped by forces outside of it, and some of it governed by habit; and with the existentialist psychologists I believe that ultimately *we* are in control of our own destiny, and that our behaviour is at times governed by a sense of purpose.

Psychology is not that different from other disciplines, many of which have lost their way. Those that claim to be saying something about human life seem to me to share two fundamental errors, or prejudices, which do nothing to help us in our search for proper self-knowledge or knowledge of others. First, they distinguish too readily between thought and emotion, which are, in fact, one and the same. As the poet Roger McGough muses on the subject of worry. 'It helps keep the brain occupied.' As a result, psychologists tend to explain behaviour in terms of one or the other, not seeming to realise that when we think we also feel, and when we feel we also think. The distinction has also encouraged the peculiar and damaging notion that men are ruled more by the brain or intellect while women are more emotional. Therefore men ought to behave in a non-emotional manner, as if showing emotion signified being out of control, irrational, less heroic. This dichotomy is so ingrained that we have partly come to believe it. We too readily forget that, as Eden Kane put it in 1964, 'Boys cry.'

The second disastrous shift that modern academic thinking has encouraged is to ignore everything that cannot be measured,

9

implying that it is either not really important or that it will somehow go away.

The consequence is that there are many pompous academics littered around the globe who are intent on changing our vocabulary of life. They do not sit down and discuss important questions such as 'What is the meaning of life?', or address themselves to vital problems that centre on human emotions and personal relationships, because such matters cannot be measured.

I believe, therefore, that we can dismiss much of what we read in academic scholarship concerning our ordinary interpersonal lives. The researchers who chop up our experience of relationships into little bits in the hope that these might be measurable are missing the point; it is our total experience, our history, the context of our life, that motivates us. Examples of this misguided approach are provided by sociobiology and social psychology – two subjects which seem totally to ignore the fact that we are *cultural products*. The way we feel, think, see ourselves and others, behave, is always affected by the times in which we live.

Edward O. Wilson is not plastic

Sociobiology is the discipline that studies the evolution of social behaviour by combining social and biological science. Edward O. Wilson, the guru of sociobiology, claims that *Homo sapiens* – you and I – shares with other social mammals certain tendencies, as, for example, male dominance systems, sexual division of labour, prolonged maternal care and extended socialisation among the young. Human variations, he adds, are 'most notable in the details of language, technology, and fashion'. Indeed he asserts that human behaviour is 'dominated by culture' in the sense that the variation between societies is based mainly on differences in cultural experience. Nonetheless, Wilson concludes:

'This is not to say that human beings are infinitely plastic. Even during periods of relative isolation human societies did not drift apart in the manner of stars in an expanding universe. When compared with the thousands of other social species, human beings can be seen to operate within limits.'

It is this kind of thinking – that we operate 'within limits', implying that we are somehow 'programmed' – which leads to the justification of such patterns of behaviour as male dominance. In fact, we can do *almost* anything we like; our destiny is in *our* hands, and does not reside in some deep and mysterious biological imperative.

The limitations of the sociobiological approach can also be seen when dealing with the question of mate selection. David Barash, for example, arguing that the 'major biological function of man-woman pair-bonding is the production of successful offspring', adds that 'love, companionship, and sexual satisfaction can all be seen as proximate means of achieving this ultimate end'. This notion is as restrictive as the forms of Christian ideology which claim that the sole function of sexual behaviour and sexual experience is reproduction. Barash appears to have forgotten the whole history of contraception, the development of test-tube technology, and other factors which have made us creatures who can (and do) engage in sexual activity almost continuously for *pleasure*. Barash also argues that as 'human behaviour has been selected to maximise inclusive fitness', we might expect to see evidence of this in mate selection. In other words, 'selection' would favour those individuals opting for mates who conferred 'maximum reproductive success' upon the discriminating partner, and that 'individuals are most fit if they make the best choice'. One might predict, therefore, a positive correlation between physical viability, general health and other indicators of reproductive potential in either sex, 'those characteristics perceived as attractive by members of the opposite sex', such as 'regularity of features, smoothness of complexion, optimum stature (neither too short nor too tall), good physique . . . '

What Barash and other sociobiologists appear to be saying is that there is a deep biological pattern to the partly random and often mysterious game of mate selection. They are arguing that at some mega-unconscious level we somehow 'choose' our partners by virtue of factors out of our control. In other words, we're not *choosing* at all. And Barash is also saying that the fit – for argument's sake, the beautiful and the healthy – choose the fit, not by chance, but in order to maintain the health of the population. This is not only nonsense, it also implies a 'desire' or imperative within us to produce a *pure* and healthy population. Few would deny that in the jungle 'fitness' is important, but in our modern societies the weak and the unattractive can and do survive. Hence they are regularly chosen as partners for companionship, for sex, for love, and often for life.

Another sociobiological line of non-reasoning concerns the patterns and forms of relationships in which we engage. Robert Hinde, for example, argues that many characteristics of human marriage systems can be viewed in relation to a polygynous tendency, or in terms of serial monogamy. In other words, we men are forced continually to seek and compete for females, because of a compulsive desire or need for more than one partner. As I have suggested, such sociobiological thinking *justifies* our behaviour, it does *not* explain it.

Unlike you and me, Edward O. Wilson is *not* plastic. He is not a free man because he has bought an illusion, the illusion that we are fundamentally related to non-human animals in a significant sense. It is dangerous to believe in sociobiology and its bedfellows, appealing though they may be. I greatly enjoy Desmond Morris as well-written and amusing fiction. But we must avoid any tendency to explain our chosen behaviour, culturally formed though it is, in terms of what animals may have been doing for centuries. If we go out on a Saturday night and behave like members of a marauding pack of wild dogs, it is because we *want* to. Don't blame my pet monkey.

The feminist, May Sarton, in her moving diary entitled *Journal of a Solitude*, puts the differences well when she asks rhetorically:

'Does anything in nature despair except man? An animal with a foot caught in a trap does not seem to despair. It is too busy trying to survive. It is all closed in, to a kind of still, intense waiting. Is this a key? Keep busy with survival. Imitate the trees. Learn to lose in order to recover, and remember that nothing stays the same for long, not even pain, psychic pain. Sit it out. Let it all pass. Let it go.'

In other words, we humans have the capacity to reflect upon our condition, change our behaviour, learn, if we so wish, to think and act differently. Most psychological research and thinking on the subject of love, sexual attraction and mate selection tends, like sociobiology, to portray us as totally determined creatures, victims of those mysterious and hard to describe individual differences that define our personalities.

Psychos

In my opinion, the death of Freud virtually heralded the death of psychology. Blinkered though Freud may have been, the box of tricks that he described and called the mind, consisting of our childhood experiences, our sexual battles, our unconscious urges and our environmental pressures, was the nearest we'll ever get to self-understanding. The fact that we know so little about ourselves is no mystery. Freud explained it. We are all incomplete and struggling creatures capable of memorable moments of self-delusion. Put us all together, toss in some culture, and you have a recipe for madness, variously called society or civilisation.

I am against all forms of pseudo-knowledge that claim to be telling us significant facts which turn out on inspection to be vacuous. Social psychology, especially in its modern form, constantly does this. Take the case of Drs Wilson and Nias in their encouragingly titled book *Love's Mysteries*. They claim that as a 'general rule' sexual attraction is based on the differences between the sexes, that consequently 'the points of maximum difference will be the most attractive and arousing', and therefore that 'the more exaggerated these differences, within reason, the more sexually attractive they will be'. Sexual attractiveness in women, claim our intrepid truth seekers, 'is magnified by large breasts and hips set against a narrow waist', which exaggerates the way in which 'the average female form diverges from that of the male'. Obviously our good doctors have been so busy that they have been unable to catch the cultural changes going on around them. They continue to argue that 'introverts' – maybe you and me – are likely to feel 'overwhelmed by nude and well-developed women and feel more at ease with thin and thoughtful-looking girls'. Furthermore, 'men who liked large-breasted women tended to be *Playboy* readers, smokers, sportsmen, being extrovert and "masculine" in their interests, whereas the men who preferred fully clothed small-breasted women were introverts, submissive, drank little alcohol and held fundamentalist religious beliefs'.

This type of 'research' is undeniably good fun, but it consistently ignores that we are cultural products, as well as being unique beings. Ted Polhemus, for example, discussing the social and cultural dimension of anorexia in *The Body Reader*, puts the argument well when he observes that while 'it was once fashionable to be as plump and "well-endowed" as ladies in paintings by Titian and Renoir, we have seen a shift towards an ideal of thinness as exemplified in the art of Klimt and Schiele and in fashion models such as Twiggy and Veruschka'. And he points out that this change in socially accepted styles has been so nearly complete that we have to pause and remind ourselves that in other societies and historical periods girls who looked like Twiggy, for example, or more recently Jerry Hall, would have had to resign themselves either to camouflage or to staying at home. Indeed, quite recently in certain parts of West Africa, fathers who could afford to do so traditionally sent their daughters to 'fattening-houses' where they were kept in seclusion, fed on fatty foods and allowed no physical exertion, so that after a year or more they would emerge pale and plump to the point of dangerous obesity. And how can anyone ignore the realities of the androgynous imagery which has developed over the past couple of decades? It may be that in the final analysis, as they say, we reach beyond the image, the cultural product, and meet the 'real' person. I doubt it, as I will argue later. But we cannot dismiss the potency of these changing cultural stereotypes. They determine, to a large degree, our definitions of self and others.

I believe that there is practically nothing new or revealing to be learned from psychological research about love, romance, mate selection and sexual behaviour. Take the question of whether opposites attract each other or whether like appeals to like. Psychologists cannot agree on the matter although most of them proclaim that it is important for successful relationships that a couple share similar values and world-views. Such vacuous and obvious conclusions would not be so depressing if it weren't for the resources, effort and belief that have gone into such work.

The American-imported soap opera *Psychos*, an everyday story of the scientific community at work, is quite revealing . . .

At the University of Muskegon, located on the edge of Lake Michigan, two psychologists, Drs Goldberg and Anderson, are working on a matter of crucial scientific importance . . .

Dr Michael Goldberg	Larry, I believe we are now in a position to test the hypothesis.
Dr Larry Anderson	Really?
Goldberg	Yes . . .
Anderson (*anxiously*)	Are you sure?
Goldberg (*assertively*)	I've never been more certain.
Anderson (*vigorously*)	Well, let's go for it.
Goldberg	What do you mean 'let's go for it', Larry?
Anderson (*jauntily*)	Oh, it's just a term I picked up when I appeared in that documentary on the psychology of left-handed people. You know the work I did on the sexual preferences of left-handed people . . . Left-handed men prefer women with glasses . . .
Goldberg (*interrupting*)	Yes, yes . . .

Seven psychology students, three males and four females, are sitting at desks piled high with pictures of men and women. Strapped to their wrists are electrodes. Sitting a little distance away are the doctors, sifting through piles of questionnaires. Dr Anderson has a box on his lap with a switch and green light on the top.

Anderson	Any idea how this works, Michael?
Goldberg	Haven't a clue. Tweak the switch . . .
Male student (*offscreen*)	Christ, fuck me, what's going on? . . . (*thump*).
Anderson	Michael, pick him up. At least I know how it works now.

Dr Goldberg instructs the students as to their duties.

Goldberg	We know you. We *know* you. We really

	do. Your answers to the nine hundred questions set out in the 'Muskegon Personality Profile Inventory' have provided us with the data we needed to understand you, for your personality profile . . .
Anderson (*overlapping*)	Why was yours late in arriving, Rosenblum?
Goldberg	Larry. Larry. Ssh. As I was saying . . . your personality profile allows us to predict which type of face, physique and part of body you prefer in the opposite sex. So when you view the pictures before you, rank them one to ten in terms of attraction. Perhaps, Larry, you'd like to explain the technology?
Anderson	Well, we know some of you inevitably will be shy. Coy. You'll feel unable to tell the truth, what you really feel about the pictures, the flesh, the *breasts, legs,* . . .

Dr Anderson, visibly shaken and perspiring considerably, retreats from the laboratory and into the lavatory.

Goldberg	Sorry. Male menopause. What he was going to say is that we'll assist you, encourage you, prod you to make your decisions, your rankings, if you look . . . look indecisive, unsure, overcome, shy. Fine . . . oh here's Dr Anderson.
Anderson	Sorry Michael.
Goldberg	It's okay Larry. I *do* understand.

One hour later.
Dr Goldberg stands over one of the students, Rosenblum.

Goldberg	Look, Chuck – you don't mind if I call you Chuck?
Rosenblum (*overlapping*)	Feel free.
Goldberg	Well, Chuck, as I was saying, you are a 'legs man'.
Rosenblum (*puzzled*)	A 'legs man'?
Goldberg	Yes, a 'legs man'. Breasts don't mean a great deal to you. Neither does . . .
Anderson (*offscreen*)	. . . ass . . .
Goldberg	Quite.
Rosenblum	So what?
Goldberg	'So what?' The point is, Chuck, that you've ranked her (*points to picture*) above her (*points to picture*). But she's just breasts, as opposed to her (*points to picture*), who you've ranked lower, who has long, thin, delicious legs.
Rosenblum	So what?
Goldberg (*angrily*)	Because she (*points to picture*) should be ranked higher, bimbo! That's what!
Rosenblum (*angrily*)	But I *prefer* Dolly Parton!
Goldberg (*angrily*)	No you don't!
Rosenblum (*shouting*)	Yes I fucking well do!
Goldberg (*shouting*)	Larry, give him some juice . . .

Scenes of horror, writhing students. Smell of burning flesh. Both doctors stand over Rosenblum.

Goldberg (*quietly*)	Chuck. Chuck. Can you hear me?
Rosenblum (*groaning*)	Uugh . . .
Goldberg	You *do* rank Dolly lower . . . don't you, *really*?
Rosenblum (*sighing*)	Yes. Yes. I do.

The doctors are in a local bar. Budweiser neon signs flash on and off. Anderson is animated.

17

Anderson	Michael, we've done it. I can't wait to write up the results. We have a *type*. 'Legs men' are always below six feet; always slightly overweight; invariably Caucasian; prefer Gore Vidal to Tom Wolfe; well–educated up to college level; heavy drinkers; from emotionally deprived backgrounds . . . oh I can't wait to see it in the *Journal* . . .
Goldberg	Well you won't have to wait too long.
Anderson (*puzzled*)	What do you mean?
Goldberg (*smiling*)	Next week.
Anderson (*aghast*)	Next week?
Goldberg	Got it in one.
Anderson	But we've only just done the experiment . . .
Goldberg (*interrupting*)	I wrote the piece last year in my sabbatical term . . . in New York.
Anderson (*angrily*)	You made it up! How could you . . . what if the experiment didn't work out?
Goldberg	But it did Larry, it *did*.
Anderson	But what . . .
Goldberg (*chuckling*)	Who checks, Larry, who checks? (*Both laugh*).
Anderson	A *type*, a *type*, Michael. We've invented a *type*.
Goldberg (*smiling*)	Yes, we'll be in the textbooks soon.
Anderson (*looks upward*)	A life in the textbooks . . .

Both slightly drunk, they kiss, then leave hand in hand and return to their love nest.

END

More recent psychological research has concentrated more on the *skills* apparently required to make relationships work. Steve Duck, in his *Friends, For Life: the psychology of close relationships*, writes: 'Friend–

ships do not just happen; they have to be made – made to start, made to work, made to develop, kept in good working order, and preserved from going sour.' This, in fact, is a new version of Karel Capek's robots. In Capek's *R.U.R.* (Rossum's Universal Robots), published in 1920, the robots kill practically everyone and man is ultimately redeemed only because, through the miracle of love, the machines are transformed into human beings. Dr Duck considers we are incapable of muddling through relationships like others before us. Here we are being deluged by more technological advice on how to keep the machine functioning. Obviously there is plenty to learn about relationships, but reducing them to the level of robotic activities is taking it too far. Besides, it assumes that relationships are based on decisions, on intellect, on logistics; whereas, in fact, they are altogether more irrational, emotional and compulsive.

Dr Duck's account diminishes the uniqueness of ourselves and our relationships, seeking to replace it with textbook formulae. He argues that people who have no friends are not social and personal failures, but 'probably just not performing the behaviours of friendship in a properly polished manner'. What *is* he talking about? Don't we all know people who, far from being 'polished', are clumsy, indeed inept, but often greatly liked? Anyway, Duck elaborates and suggests that to develop a close friendship with someone who 'used to be a stranger' we have to perform a number of tasks. 'We have to assess the other person accurately, adopt appropriate styles of communication and bodily posture, and find out how to satisfy mutual personality needs; we have to learn to adjust our behaviour to the other person and to select and reveal the right sorts of information or opinions in an inviting, encouraging way in the appropriate style and circumstances; we have to build up trust, to make suitable demands and build up commitment . . . ' How can anyone write like this? I refuse to be conceived of as a robot. In any case, the interpersonal map is populated by people *in* relationships who are always behaving inappropriately but who nonetheless get along. But let us take a more detailed look at what Dr Duck is proposing.

Lesson number one: The very first stage in making friendships is what the author calls 'ecology of attraction', a grasp of the situations and circumstances in which attraction is 'permitted' and also of the places or occasions when it is not. We usually 'try to meet liked people more often in places where food and drink are served . . . disliked people are encountered in places where work is done . . . ' and 'liked people are met for longer periods of time and the meeting is usually less structured or focused than is a meeting with someone we dislike'. In other words: we do not date people on the top of mountains or in sinking ships; we ask people's names and get friendly if they take their clothes off; there are no such things as hospital romances or student lovers; and we don't keep our trousers on when she removes her knickers.

Lesson number two: 'The ability to recognise when, even in the right circumstances, the other person is resistant to entering a relationship'. In other words, he's referring to those memorable occasions when we approach the woman of our dreams: 'Hi, I'm Jim, can I speak to you? This is a good place for conversation, it's not a mountain top.' 'Get lost, creep!' Duck claims firstly that people only tend to go for people similar to themselves – 'men may desire attractive looking women more often than unattractive ones, but are more nervous of approaching them and experience high fears of rejection' – and secondly that 'people who have frequently experienced rejection in the past, and who blame themselves for it, are likely to maintain low drives towards friendship through fears of further humiliation'. Has Dr Duck never encountered masochists? And has he never played the game of 'I bet you can't pull her', and subsequently been pleasantly surprised? No, his account, as well as being alarmingly sexist, is based on some mythical notion of *normality.* I happen to believe that masochism is as normal a pattern of behaviour as altruism or sadism. But Dr Duck does not let us in to *his* definition of normality.

Lesson number three: 'At certain ages a person is more likely to be searching for particular sorts of relationships and is more likely to be active in attempts to expand his social network.' Or, put simply, Methuselah doesn't go to singles bars or discotheques.

Lesson number four: 'The first couple of minutes of conversation with someone are points where they attempt to get across to others the central features of their "person" as they see it.' Duck describes

20

such minutes as absolutely significant. But are they? Haven't we all loathed someone initially, drifted in and out of conversation with them, but later thought 'mmmm'? Besides, we all know that the first few minutes is an ad, a promo, and invariably far from truthful. Mind you, it doesn't stop academics going to Berlin for the fourth world congress on 'the significance of the first seven words in the formation of stable marital bonds among the Eskimo'.

Lesson number five: 'We all draw inferences about someone's personality from the way that they look, and too often these judgements are sweeping, general and unhelpful'; for example, we assume 'inward deviance from an outwardly deviant appearance', that, for instance, 'people with scars on their cheeks are assumed to be criminals'. It is certainly true that in the interpersonal market place one can operate on physical appearance; indeed, it is hardly surprising, given the pressures of popular culture, advertising and the fashion industry. But even here we need to take into account cultural and individual differences. I know women who *only* pay attention to men with scars on their faces; I know women who go for ugly men. But in any event, what does Duck really mean when he talks of physical appearance? Beauty and ugliness *are* in the eye of the beholder. And most of us *do* know that beneath the clothing and layers of skin lies something else, often quite different.

Lesson number six: 'Friendship is not just like a light bulb waiting for a person with the right characteristics to come and switch it on.' Rather, the development of friendship occurs through 'the skills of partners in revealing or disclosing their attitudes first and later their personalities, inner character and true selves'. Getting to know you, in other words. But apparently this has to be done in a 'reciprocal manner, turn-by-turn, and in a way that keeps pace with the revelations and disclosures made by the partner'. Although this has the ring of truth to it, it rests once again on the notion of 'normal man'. I happen to love the woman I live with but still know nothing about her. She doesn't disclose too much about herself. Why should she? Besides, if she did, I might not like what I heard. As for me, I prattle on endlessly and reveal *all*; the trouble is she's not in the same room at the time, and besides, I haven't as yet found my 'true self'.

21

When our psychologist meets Ralph, Jack and Piggy . . .

I'm nearly through with Dr Duck, but please bear with me, as some of his final thoughts *are* interesting. He turns to children's friendships as the roots to success or otherwise in adult relationships. So far, so good. He makes the very apt point that the parent who 'devotes energy to creating in the very young child a favourable self-image is doing that child at least as much good as a parent who devotes time to teaching the child to read at an early age'. More so, in fact. Children with a well-developed sense of self-esteem – 'I matter, I count, I am worthwhile' – are better prepared to cope with possible rejection, prompting the hurt cry of 'you're not my best friend any more'. Once again, however, Duck over-emphasises his point in arguing that for children, learning to make friends is 'something that has to be acquired, learned carefully, and practised'. But learning and practising do not necessarily lead to the formation of friendships. Some children base friendships on excessive dependence, some on exploitation, and others on a natural flair for popularity.

Most of us experience difficulties in childhood relationships, feel sad and bitter, get over them, muddle along, but never really forget the past. Not only do the recollections of those problems, pains and pleasures remain; the child also stays *within* us. Childhood *is* full of disappointments and is brutish as well as joyous. But isn't that simply how it is and always has been? Even if it were possible, would we want it more planned? The agonies of childhood either emotionally cripple us or make us the incomplete but lovable adults we are.

2

The revolt of the unoppressed and the culture of narcissism meet mainstreet drudgery

'. . . people have convinced themselves that what matters is psychic self-improvement; getting in touch with their feelings, eating health food, taking lessons in ballet or belly-dancing, immersing themselves in the wisdom of the East, jogging, learning how to "relate", overcoming the "fear of pleasure". Harmless in themselves, these pursuits, elevated to a program and wrapped in the rhetoric of authenticity and awareness, signify a retreat from politics and a repudiation of the recent past. Indeed Americans seem to wish to forget not only the sixties, the riots, the new left, the disruptions on college campuses, Vietnam, Watergate, and the Nixon presidency, but their entire collective past . . . '

Christopher Lasch

Ray Gosling in his entertaining memoir of the Sixties, *Personal Copy*, wittily recalls that 'when half the world were expanding their bodies and minds, blowing their minds out, I was panting up slate-strewn streets with a rat in a plastic bag, trying to find some pitiful councillor I could embarrass: "We've found this in Dame Agnes Street", you'd say, just as they were going into a munch.' Now Ray Gosling is no slouch, no wallflower, yet he wasn't doing at that time what everyone was *supposed* to be doing. The same goes for me. When social analysts were saying 'my generation' were into the Grateful Dead, I was into Howling Wolf; told that we were reading Hermann Hesse, I was flicking through the pages of *The L-Shaped Room*; others might be dope heads, but I was still boozing; and when informed that my generation was experimenting with sex and getting lots of it, I felt the odd one out.

This is not merely a long-winded way of saying 'we are all different'; rather to point out that it *is* important to know the type of cultural air we breathe, the changing social customs and expectations that frame our actions, the generational shifts that occur in beliefs, attitudes, ideologies and behaviour. These clearly influence what we as individuals do in our lives. But in order to make sense of such changes, we must, in the first place, try to discover the extent of such shifts, determine how many people *really* were affected, and, secondly, ask to what degree individual minds and hearts were motivated by such changes and what, therefore, was the end result for society and social relationships. In a sense, all the shifts which have occurred and which affect us *now* are focused on the primacy of *youth*, the search for self-development, identity, autonomy and 'authenticity', and the 'sexual revolution'. Of course, many people still labour under the weight of earlier cultures, notably the Victorian values of abstinence, hypocrisy and religious guilt; but for most of us, life has never been quite the same since Elvis Presley.

A musicologist may well quibble and point to the seminal influence of Bill Haley's 1954 *Shake Rattle and Roll*, and rock'n'roll undoubtedly laid the foundations of long-term change, but it was Presley's mixture of rebelliousness and sexuality that really started the ball rolling. The year 1956 produced *Heartbreak Hotel, Blue Suede Shoes, Hound Dog, Love Me Tender*, followed in 1957 by *All Shook Up* and the next year by the momentous *Jailhouse Rock*. Elvis encouraged previously timid (and tepid) youth to express their sexuality openly, to question their parents' authority, and ultimately to idolise themselves by idolising him. Obviously such attitudes were not entirely foreign to previous generations, but history does have its turning points and I believe this was one of them – minor maybe, in the context of political, economic

24

and military change, but important in terms of the cultural fabric of everyday life.

Popular music, in my opinion, is a significant pointer to cultural trends simply because it *is* popular. Modern commercial music is the voice of youth and 'ordinary people'. This is not to deny that the popular music industry is somehow connected with capitalism, materialism or consumerism, because obviously it is; nor am I suggesting that *all* the music is sexual in tone or radical in content. Indeed, the continual use of the term 'baby' – invariably by men – in songs like *Baby I Need Your Loving* or *Baby Come Back*, tends to reduce women to the status of juveniles, which is certainly not a progressive or radical message. Nevertheless, it has become the *potentially* liberating means of expression and escape for discontented, frustrated, expectant people in their millions.

Presley, along with Chuck Berry and Buddy Holly, prepared the ground for the arrival of *Beatlemania*. There has been nothing quite like it; millions of sexually aroused youngsters around the globe letting go, and giving vent to their desires. Especially important was the fact that girls and women too could scream for sex at men on public display. This period of 1962 to 1965 heralded a worldwide search for physical identity, proclaimed most conspicuously in the area of mass-market fashion, setting a trend which, despite subsequent variations, has never waned. Sexual pleasure was the order of the day. The following period, 1967-8, variously described in terms of the 'student revolution' the 'counter-culture' and 'flower power', was the most important in post-war years.

From the vantage point of the materialistic and politically vicious Eighties, the Sixties and its 'counter-culture' tend to be dismissed as make-believe – a time of self-indulgence, disorientation, bewilderment and irresponsibility. But is this a valid judgement? Exactly what was this counter-culture? Clearly it involved a substantial and influential proportion of young people. Yet the 'movement' was not confined – as some have alleged – to the college-educated upper middle classes. It also had some effect upon young wage-earners from a less privileged background. Certainly there was widespread disagreement as to its significance. The historians Frank and Fritzie Manuel (*Utopian Thought in the Modern World*) dismiss the counter-

culture as a 'potpourri of outworn conceptions – a bit of transcendence, body mysticism, sexual freedom, the abolition of work, the
end of alienation'. Theodore Roszak, in *The Making of the Counter
Culture*, saw it rather differently, arguing that middle-class youth had
grasped the fact that the 'paramount struggle of our day is against . . .
technocracy', the undesirable consequences of progress. So what
form did this struggle take? For the counter-culture (as opposed to the
other strand, the counter-politic, if you like) it was an attempt to
reject materialism, consumerism, competitiveness and violence. This
rejection was manifested in a reluctance to engage in traditional work
– or as Richard Neville put it, in *Playpower*: 'Work = Castration. Join
the gentle strike . . . ' – and more involvement with drugs, drugs-
related music and sexuality. And, arguably, more emotion and
openness.

On the subject of drugs, Richard Neville also observed that 'lateral
thinking, mystical drifters rarely maim other people', while pop-
artist Andy Warhol recollected *his* Sixties, noting that 'during this
period I took thousands of Polaroids of genitals. Whenever somebody
came to the factory, no matter how straight-looking he was, I'd ask
him to take his pants off so I could photograph his cock and balls.'
People undoubtedly *did* take more drugs than previously and with
more purpose, and both men and women appeared to indulge in more
sexual activity. But how much is more? To illustrate, let us look at
one particular day – 12 July 1967. On this day Scott McKenzie's *San
Francisco (Be sure to wear a flower in your hair)* and the Beatles' *All You
Need is Love* entered the charts, both of them anthems to the new
generation committed to 'free love'. But the charts also included
Englebert Humperdinck, Cat Stevens and the totally fabricated
Monkees. *The Times* carried no stories about 'free love' or the
impending revolution, nor advertisements for paisley-patterned
shirts; it reported riots in Hong Kong, a proposed strike by the
National Union of Teachers and the following two news items:

> *Saigon:* 'President Johnson will continue to furnish
> reinforcements requested by the American Command in
> Vietnam, but the important thing was to make better use of the
> million American and South Vietnam troops already there,' says

McNamara, American Defence Secretary.

Washington: Mr Orville Freeman, the Secretary of Agricul-
ture, today announced new measures to provide food for
millions of poor Americans. They will first be applied in Minnis-
sippi where a team of physicians recently described the nutritional and medical conditions of children as shocking . . . In
child after child [we] saw; evidence of vitamin and mineral
deficiencies . . . diseases of the heart and the lungs . . . children
afflicted with chronic diarrhoea, chronic sores, chronic leg and
arm injuries, and deformities . . . '

Indeed, the only 'new generation' story was one of a 24-year-old
murdered secretary who, we were told, was 'mini-skirted'.

There were many, including myself, who did *not* wear beads, frilly
shirts and kaftans, and who would not have been seen dead in flared
trousers. Not everyone liked Procul Harum or listened to Pink Floyd
or Jefferson Airplane. Yet few remained untouched by the times. And
even those who did not want to change the world or withdraw from it
were excited by what was happening, realising that life could be
different, that this was a time of *potential* hedonism, of fun, ultimately
of sexual gratification. The counter-politic movement, for its part,
was easier to comprehend and fundamentally more coherent,
although it too had its more frivolous side. For instance, in 1968 one
could 'Dial-A-Demonstration' and find out where the protests
around town were that day. This particular cohort of Sixties youth
engaged in struggles against American involvement in Vietnam,
against black oppression and, of course, against the French govern-
ment and other centres of power. Charles Reich, in his sympathetic
and well-meaning book, *The Greening of America*, believed that the
counter-politic signalled a 'revolution coming' which would 'orig-
inate with the individual and with culture, and it will change the
political structure only as its final act'. His 'revolution of the new
generation', as he called it, which included such acts as political
demonstrations, was essentially about a 'change of consciousness' and
the development of 'a new man'. Reich was wildly optimistic, but
again not totally wrong.

It is probably true that the disparate totality of the counter-culture

27

ended in disarray, yet its influence has been both positive and lasting, albeit somewhat diluted. The counter-politic strand suffered a worse defeat. It has helped to transform politics but not in the manner desired. Governments and centres of power have asserted themselves more forcibly, while on the other side of the barricades, so to speak, disillusionment has set in. This has had many long-term negative consequences, culminating in a general retreat.

The activists of the counter-culture helped to provide a blueprint for other young people, giving future generations a sense of freedom, identity and importance. The enthusiasm and ecstasy could not be sustained – age would see to that. But it was a heady time and the message has never been entirely lost.

When precisely did the Sixties end? Joan Didion, discussing in *The White Album* the murder of Sharon Tate by Charles Manson and his maniacs, argued: 'Many people I knew in Los Angeles believe that the Sixties ended abruptly on August 9, 1969, ended at the exact moment when word of the murders on Cielo Drive travelled like a bush fire through the community, and in a sense this is true.' Presumably what she meant was that the occasional contemporary examples of extreme behaviour, extreme beliefs and extreme experimentation had to come to an end because of their consequences. It had all gone too far. The Seventies and Eighties have certainly been different. The search for identity has continued, the emphasis on fashion has become even more exaggerated, music has remained central, political activism has declined, and there has been a fundamental trend towards social withdrawal and a consequent preoccupation with *self*.

The mainstream social and cultural analysts have characterised the two decades since the Sixties as periods of social disengagement, impotence, despair and introspection. Tom Wolfe has talked of the 'me decade', Lasch of the 'culture of narcissism', while Richard Sennett has lamented the 'fall of public man'. Symptomatic of this mood has been the eager search for self-identity and self-fulfilment as seen in the growth of the new quasi-religions, the human potential and 'body beautiful' movements, obsessions about health and alternative medicine, rampant consumerism, privatisation, and the decline of interest in the public sphere. Wolfe, Lasch and Sennett have viewed this changing mood as morally objectionable, ultimately self-defeating and potentially apolitical, although Lasch has argued that disillusion with establishment politics is, in fact, a sign of increased public awareness. These and other writers have contrasted these decades unfavourably with the period of the Sixties which, for all its posturing, was at least an assertion of hope. Edwin Schur, another critic of the period, is appalled by the widespread incidence of self-preoccupation, which runs counter to social change, complaining that 'white middle-class awareness enthusiasts amuse themselves with yoga and body relaxation, at the indirect expense of blacks, Chicanos, and American Indians – whose real suffering is being ignored'.

If 'free love' was the standard of that small band of Sixties activists, 'self-awareness' and 'meaningful relationships' are the symbolic keywords of the opinion moulders and activists of the 'new narcissism'. This mood should not be dismissed as merely elitist. Working-class men jog, factory girls do yoga and aerobics, parents are conscious of the need to give their children a healthy diet, and there is enormous public interest in such topics as astrology, Tarot-card reading and meditation. But this does not imply that such individuals are quite unconcerned about politics, community affairs and other people. More probably they have developed a little more self-knowledge and awareness, and perhaps keener psychological sensibilities. So why the criticism?

Well, some people argue that the new moods of narcissism have placed considerable stress on private intimate relationships, so that even the family can be accused of being a tyrannical institution. Certainly the neurotic male cries of 'was it good for you?' are more frequently heard nowadays, but is that so bad? Deeper knowledge of the relationships, patterns and feelings that occur within ourselves and our families surely helps to avoid the many pitfalls to which we are prone. Martin Gross, however, widens the context and believes that the current moods, of which he is critical, redefine normality and take the 'painful reactions to the normal vicissitudes of life – despair, anger, frustration and label them as maladjustments'. Gross adds that the 'semantic trick is in the equating of happiness with normality'.

'By permitting this, we have given up our simple right to be both *normal* and *suffering* at the same time. Instead, we have

29

massively redefined ourselves as *neurotic*, even as incipient mental cases, particularly when life plays its negative tricks. It is a tendency which gives modern America, and increasingly much of the Western world, the tone of a giant psychiatric clinic.'

Our alleged self-preoccupation is reflected by the increasingly therapeutic environment in which we live. The civilised and cultured yuppies (as opposed to the merely money-grabbing yuppies) certainly seem to show some interest in 'finding themselves'. Although fads such as *est*, encounter groups, bioenergetics and the like are now on the decline, the vocabulary of these movements has seeped into the cultural air we breathe. Ordinary people with no involvement in psychology or psychiatry talk of 'needing space', of 'relating to' others, of their need to take 'responsibility for themselves'. Now that the almost comic-strip cosmology of the pure therapies and the associated remedies such as the 'new religions' have virtually disappeared, we seem to be left with a healthy quest for self-knowledge, even though at times in conversation it can become very boring.

My own involvement in the 'new therapies and the search for self' was secondhand rather than direct. In 1982-3 I spent some time at a commune whose members were seeking such things as love and truth, under the auspices of Bhagwan Shree Rajneesh. In the Seventies and Eighties he developed notoriety as the 'sex guru' – partly on the basis of his book *From Sex to Superconsciousness* in which he claimed you could 'glimpse God through sexual ecstasy', and partly because of his emphasis on the value of sexually based therapies. After some years of financial wheeling and dealing, including his establishment of a Rajneesh 'city' in Oregon, USA, he now lives in semi-exile in India. In this particular commune there was a centre for alternative medicine, various types of individual and group therapy, massage treatment, Tarot card reading and re-birthing. The commune members were undoubtedly well-intentioned, determined to live *their* way, not by tradition or dictate. But I always felt it was rather illusory, that one day they would be compelled to re-enter the 'real world', full of its conflicts, warts and endless compromises. Just as I prefer the city to the country, I am inclined to choose the gigantic melting pot rather than the small club or community. That is precisely the point made by critics such as Christopher Lasch and Richard Sennett, namely that much of modern behaviour is selfish and privatised, that it denies human reciprocity and community, and is ultimately self-defeating. Let me expand.

Christopher Lasch, in his important book *The Culture of Narcissism*, argues that as the twentieth century approaches its end, the conviction grows that many other things are ending too:

'Impending disaster has become an everyday concern, so commonplace and familiar that nobody any longer gives such thought to how disaster might be averted. People busy themselves instead with survival strategies, measures designed to prolong their own lives, or programs guaranteed to ensure good health and peace of mind . . . those who dig bomb shelters hope to survive by surrounding themselves with the latest products of modern technology. Communards in the country adhere to an opposite plan: to free themselves from dependence on technology and thus to outlive its destruction or collapse.'

Most significantly, Lasch argues that both strategies reflect the growing despair of changing society, even of understanding it; this accounts for the current cults of expanded consciousness, health and personal 'growth'. In essence, 'after the political turmoil of the sixties, Americans have retreated to purely personal preoccupations'. Having more or less renounced the hope of significantly improving their lives, people have convinced themselves that what matters is psychic self-improvement. Lasch believes that contemporary 'psychological man', plagued by anxiety, depression and vague discontent, feeling a sense of inner emptiness, seeks neither individual self-aggrandisement nor spiritual transcendence but rather peace of mind, under conditions that ironically tend to militate against it. Referring primarily to the USA, Lasch asserts that modern man turns to the therapist as the principal ally in his struggle for composure, hoping thus to achieve the new equivalent of salvation, 'mental health'.

31

Lasch's fear is that 'having displaced religion as the organising framework of American culture, the therapeutic outlook threatens to displace politics as well'. He is all too aware that the radicalism of the Sixties failed to address itself to the quality of personal life, in the somewhat mistaken belief that questions of individual growth could wait until 'after the revolution'. So he is not surprised at what has come to pass.

Nonetheless, there are ironies. The 'new left' did, in fact, *begin* to address the issue; there *was* a growing recognition that personal crisis is in itself a political issue. Any thoroughgoing analysis of modern society and politics would therefore have to explain among other things, why individual growth and development are so difficult to accomplish: 'why the fear of growing up and ageing haunt our society; why personal relations have become so brittle and precarious; and why the "inner life" no longer offers any refuge from the danger around us.' Yet the biggest irony is that the very people who were beginning to make those personal-political connections have today turned their backs on the whole idea and could indeed be termed the 'new narcissists'.

This reality of disillusion and disengagement was vividly portrayed by Lawrence Kasdan in his 1983 movie *The Big Chill*. The film centres on the dynamics of a reunion. After the funeral of Alex Marshall, a promising physicist who was a drop-out in his mid-thirties, his friends Harold and Sarah Cooper put up the mourners for the weekend. Apart from Chloe, a girl in her early twenties who has been stranded with the Coopers since Alex, her boyfriend, committed suicide in their bathroom, they are all contemporaries who fondly remember their days at the University of Michigan. Sam, once a radical orator, is now the star of *J. T. Lancer*, an anodyne TV private-eye series; Meg has abandoned a career as a crusading defender of the under-privileged to become a wealthy contracts attorney; Michael, a journalist, writes personality profiles for the sleazy *People* magazine; Karen, a would-be writer, has married an advertising executive and started a family; and Nick, a former phone-in radio psychiatrist, is now a spaced-out drug dealer. Unmarried Meg is eager to be impregnated by one of her friends during the weekend, but Nick proves unapproachable, Sam turns her down, and Michael doesn't appeal. Pete, a local cop, picks up Nick, but lets him off because of his friendship with Harold. Attempting to impress Pete with one of his TV stunts, Sam slightly injures himself. Sarah, who once had a brief affair with Alex, encourages Harold to sleep with Meg. Sam and Karen, who have always been attracted, are disappointed when they finally make love. Nick and Chloe are drawn together, and decide to stay on in Alex's cottage. As the guests prepare to leave, Michael jokingly tells the Coopers that they have taken a vote and decided to stay forever. Kasdan paints his characters – originally the campus-revolt generation – as people who know they have 'sold out' and feel only dissatisfaction and guilt. They 'know' that once they were free, heroic and untainted, with aspirations to 'change the world', but now they see themselves as successful failures, individuals who have lost their way, and their souls, on the journey.

In general terms, Christopher Lasch maintains that the earlier conquest of nature and the yearning for new frontiers have given way to the search for self-fulfilment; that this self-absorption defines the moral climate of contemporary society; that 'narcissism' has become one of the central themes of contemporary culture. He argues, however, that by over-simplifying the opposition between 'real' issues and personal issues we may ignore the fact that social questions are also personal questions, and that our individual and family experiences are moulded by the real world and also colour our perception of it. Lasch concludes that the trouble with the new narcissism or consciousness movement is not that it addresses trivial or unreal issues but that it provides self-defeating solutions: 'Arising out of a pervasive dissatisfaction with the quality of personal relations, it advises people not to make too large an investment in love and friendship, to avoid excessive dependence on others, and to live for the moment – the very conditions that created the crisis of personal relations in the first place.'

Richard Sennett, in *The Fall of Public Man*, partly shares Lasch's views, but more forcefully and critically argues that a 'tyranny of intimacy' threatens to produce a total incapacity to transform the structure of modern societies. He is concerned that essentially public

33

social issues have become reduced solely to private, personal problems. The twin forces of capitalism and secularism have transformed the public arena into an inhuman and vaguely menacing presence. One response has been to withdraw into a private world in order to create an infrastructure of so-called authenticity. However, what begins as a human aspiration becomes self-defeating since the original problem is not solved, merely avoided. Social fulfilment is to be achieved by rendering the public private, so that intimacy becomes an attempt to solve what is essentially a public problem by denying that the public element exists. For Sennett this is the greatest mystification of all. He summarises his argument as follows:

'The reigning belief today is that closeness between persons is a moral good. The reigning aspiration of today is to develop individual personality through experiences of closeness and warmth with others. The reigning myth today is that the evils of society can all be understood as evils of impersonality, alienation and coldness.'

In Sennett's view, the 'tyranny of intimacy' becomes a political catastrophe as it leads to the denial of the public realm; narcissistic self-absorption leads only to political immobility.

What, you may ask, has all this to do with you and me? Just consider. There is certainly some truth in the Lasch/Sennett scenario. People of all classes persist in their high expectations of personal relationships yet stress the importance of individual independence. They have become more private and increasingly disenchanted with politics. The grim reality of widescale unemployment ensures that people are increasingly worried about their future and are therefore less likely to rebel and to voice their discontent publicly. Another reason why it is important to heed the messages is that even if you or I haven't booked into Hotel Narcissism, the people we meet may well have done.

Times have certainly changed. I am more concerned than ever about my image and self identity; I am a Filofax-carrying, designer-

34

coated socialist. I encounter daily the vocabulary of 'authenticity and justice in relationships'. I am constantly scolded for eating white bread and for not jogging. I continue to consume large quantities of alcohol in an attempt to imagine another world, if only temporarily, to pursue hedonism, sex and 'romantic love', and to take an interest in politics. Today's music also tells us that things have changed. Bruce Springsteen now sings songs of male tenderness, as Bob Dylan did a generation earlier; yet the images created by 'pop video' have come to assume even greater importance than the music itself. Perhaps, though, it is the smooth, sexual and contrived pseudo-awareness of the hugely successful George Michael that underlines the difference between this generation and earlier ones.

Analysts other than Lasch and Sennett, however, welcome recent changes and believe them to be a positive force for cultural change. Daniel Yankelovich, for example, in his wonderfully titled *New Rules: searching for self-fulfilment in a world turned upside down*, believes that the search for self-fulfilment is actually about autonomy, creativity and material well-being, of which he approves. He sees the development of an 'embryonic ethic', centrally concerned with the formation of closer, deeper and more meaningful relationships. Marshall Colman, on the other hand, believes we have to understand the importance of *self-love*, and indeed to embrace it. For if we do not love ourselves, he argues, it is unlikely we can love others, since 'those who make harsh demands on themselves usually make harsh demands on others as well'. Colman also believes there is a case to be made *against* altruism in the sense of it being a commitment to social ideals that constantly overlooks individuals and *their* needs and weaknesses. Arlie Russell Hochschild, in her discussion of 'emotional labour' – the occupational self-presentation of smiling, for example, practised constantly by air hostesses and the like – makes the same point, if somewhat differently. In her view, the narcissist 'feeds insatiably on interactions, competing desperately for love and admiration in a Hobbesian dog-eat-dog world where both are perpetually scarce'. Such efforts are self-perpetuating because he must 'discount the results: what admiration he does receive, after all, is offered to his false self, not his real one.' Hochschild continues:

'But our culture has produced another form of false self: the altruist, the person who is overly concerned with the needs of *others*. In our culture, women – because they have traditionally been assigned the task of tending to the needs of others – are in greater danger of overdeveloping a false self and losing track of its boundaries. If developing a narcissistic false self is the greater danger for men, developing an altruistic false self is the greatest danger for women. Whereas the narcissist is adept at turning the social uses of feeling to his own advantage, the altruist is more susceptible to being used – not because her sense of self is weaker but because her "true self" is bonded more securely to the group and its welfare.'

Yankelovich, Colman and Hochschild all believe in the individual – and in the right of everyone to *be* individual. However, for our purposes, the most pertinent analysis is that of Francesca Cancian in *Love in America: Gender and Self-Development* (1987). Discussing the changes already described as the culture of narcissism, she notes the widespread belief, for example, that family relations and marriages have been strained to breaking point by the 'self-centredness of recent decades'. The implication here is that in order to strengthen close relationships we must check self-development and reassert the importance of enduring commitments and reciprocity. Cancian does not agree with the conclusion that the bonds of family and marriage fundamentally conflict with self-development. She believes in a third possibility, a 'new image of love that combines enduring love with self-development', which indeed has already emerged: 'Many Americans believe that to develop their individual potential, they need a supportive, intimate relationship with their spouse or lover', and moreover that these people see self-development and love as mutually reinforcing, not conflicting. In this image, love and self-development both grow from the mutual *interdependence* of two people, not from extreme independence, nor from the one-way dependency of a woman on a man as encouraged by traditional marriage. Cancian schematically chronicles the major changes, as she sees them, in the following way:

	Who is responsible for love?	What is love?
Feminised love		
Family Duty (nineteenth century)	woman	fulfil duty to family
Companionship (1920–)	woman	intimacy in marriage
Androgynous love		
Independence	woman and man	individual self-development and intimacy
Interdependence (1970–)	woman and man	mutual self-development, intimacy and support

From Cancian, *Blueprints of Love* (1987)

Cancian makes the point that the apparent conflict between love and self-development is linked to the 'polarisation of gender roles'. Our conception of self-development, with the attendant emphasis on aggressive independence and separation, has been masculinised, while love has been feminised. She explains:

'The dominant definition of love in our culture is feminised. Love is identified with women and with qualities seen as feminine, such as tenderness and expressing feelings. We tend to ignore the practical, material aspects of love such as giving help or sharing activities – qualities associated with masculinity and strength. Identifying love with expressing feelings is biased towards the way women prefer to behave in a love relationship.

37

Women are more skilled and more interested than men in talking about feelings, while men are interested in giving practical help . . . '

This, she argues, results in a dualism – masculine freedom of self-development versus feminine attachment to others. She is, of course, right. This particular double standard puts women at a fundamental disadvantage. It takes numerous forms and gives rise to a range of assumptions. Women should be *expected* to face and solve the emotional problems that surface within relationships; women are less able to take control of various practical and financial matters; women *ought necessarily* to be with their children; prejudice against women in the workplace or in career structures does not really matter; and in sexual relationships, what is permissible for men is unacceptable for women.

But according to Cancian (and of course Lasch, Sennett, et al) times *are* changing, self-development *is* a primary value for both men and women and, most importantly, more 'androgynous images of love and self' are developing. She talks of more flexible gender roles, and increasing concern with private life and the expression of feelings. Americans, she observes, increasingly describe a good marriage or love relationship in terms of both 'partners communicating openly, developing an autonomous self, and working on the relationship'. In this apparently new and complex 'ideal of love' the man and woman are *equally responsible* for the relationship, both openly 'dependent on the other', and yet committed to self-development. She adds, however, that 'love is still feminised in that emotional and verbal expression are emphasised'. Furthermore, conceptions of the ideal self are also becoming more androgynous, portraying a 'developed person' as someone who combines feminine intimacy and emotional expressiveness with masculine independence and competence. This 'expanded, androgynous self' is replacing the older ideal of a 'self-made man who is independent, emotionally controlled, and econo-mically successful'. She predicts that the trend 'from role to self' will continue, that androgynous love will develop and become more important, and that this trend 'may lead us to more interdependent relationships' or 'more independence and isolation'. The outcome partly depends on 'economic and political changes in the wider society'. Quite so, but there is more to it than that. Let me expand and summarise.

Elvis Presley and the Beatles helped to usher in important cultural changes. The younger generation set out on a relentless search for identity which aimed more for sexual success than self-awareness. Since then there has been increasing emphasis on personal freedom, rebellion and the pursuit of pleasure. The 'radicalism' preached by the youth of the Sixties failed to achieve anything positive but pointed the way in the direction of an inward–looking culture. The new narciss-ism is regarded by critics as self-defeating: happiness needs other people and society, not just 'self'. Sympathisers believe, however, that it could herald a new ideal of love, a more interdependent, democratic pattern of personal relationships. But whether this will develop depends substantially on economic changes.

Take the example of John and Yoko. John was the epitome of the reformed man; after a wild past he became a model of male tenderness *and* male strength, of paternal domesticity *and* creativity. Yoko combined business acumen and independence with femininity and motherhood. But it's much easier when you have money, isn't it? Besides, and this is important, not everyone *wants* to buy the new model. For instance, at the time when so many *were* changing their lives, behaving in a more sensitive and democratic manner, many men were still using violence and coercion to 'keep women in their place'.

In the Eighties countless women are still being beaten, even killed, in their homes. Some societies actually encourage wife-beating as a man's 'right'; in others the problem is hidden away, made out to be a 'private' matter. The problem is universal, and shelters for battered women (which first appeared in 1972 in the UK and Canada) now exist in many parts of the world. In addition, the fact that people cannot handle relationships satisfactorily is clearly demonstrated by the continuing escalation of the divorce rate.

I believe that this so-called 'new ideal of love' can only be of benefit to us all. Why on earth should there be prejudice against women in marriage and other relationships? Why should she have fewer rights both in motherhood and in the workplace? And why shouldn't men be tender and loving, cry and, if need be, stay at home? These are goals that we should try to achieve, provided we do not forget that we live in society, with other people whose needs, struggles and different opinions have to be heeded.

But: all this is not going to happen merely as a result of economic and political changes in society at large. It is our *minds* that have to change. We bring to our cultural melting pot all manner of ideas and notions. One widespread belief is in the reality and importance of *romantic love*. Let's take a look at it . . .

3

'All You Need is Love' sing the Beatles – and, come to that, everyone else

'I find the idea of always being in company rather oppressive; I see life more as an affair of solitude diversified by company than an affair of company diversified by solitude.'

Philip Larkin

1957 was an interesting year. At the age of thirty-five Jack Kerouac published his *On the Road*, and the beat generation was born. Albert Camus won the Nobel Prize for literature, while the Belgian army equipped itself with German Leopard tanks. Elvis Presley sang *All Shook Up*; and following the admission of nine negro students to the Central High School at Little Rock, Arkansas, Governor Orval E. Faubus sent in the National Guard to exclude them.

Nat King Cole was also singing at the time. He followed up his earlier songs, which included the optimistic *Faith Can Move Mountains* and the passionate *Love Me As If There Were No Tomorrow*, with the now immortal *When I Fall in Love*. The first line – 'When I fall in love, it will be forever, or I'll never fall in love' – voiced one of the most important notions of romantic love, that relationships not only *will* but *ought* to last forever. This is the crucial idea which drives people to near insanity, prevents them facing the truth of their relationships,

41

and stops them changing behaviour (and partners) as they blindly continue to believe in the notion of permanence. No wonder Plato, the famous Greek cave man, referred to love as a 'grave mental disease'. We all know that with 'love' lurks danger, madness and self-delusion, albeit with rare moments of joy and fulfilment. As Billie Holiday famously put it, 'Don't threaten me with love, baby. Let's just go walking in the rain.'

For the majority of us, relationships are certainly the hub of life; and so, of course, they should be. The search for 'love', for sexual gratification, the meeting of minds, companionship and friendship, not to mention reproduction, is what makes the world go round. However, it is also a frightening path to tread, full of pain, disappointments and illusions. Tomas, the central character in Milan Kundera's *The Unbearable Lightness of Being*, stands at a window trying to recall an earlier episode. The question he is asking himself is whether or not he loved Tereza:

'But was it love? The feeling of wanting to die beside her was clearly exaggerated: he had seen her only once in his life! Was it simply the hysteria of a man who, aware deep down of his inaptitude for love, felt the self-deluding need to simulate it? His unconscious was so cowardly that the best partner it could choose for its little comedy was this miserable provincial waitress with practically no chance at all to enter his life! . . . looking out over the courtyard at the dirty walls, he realised he had no idea whether it was hysteria or love.'

Do *any of us* know when we're 'in love'? We all believe we understand what love is, protesting that it is a state or condition which cannot adequately be described. But are we certain that we know what we're talking about? I doubt it.

Romantic love and its discontents

The concept of romantic love and the quest for it very frequently invades our consciousness and influences our behaviour. At best it leads to divorce or long-term boredom (also known as a 'happy marriage'): at worst it can spiral us into lunacy or even dump us into the abyss. I am not joking. Although a lucky few survive the illusion and create some form of happiness for themselves, people do kill because of 'love'.

Hardly a day passes without a popular piece of music being released about romantic love, the search for the perfect partner and the accompanying heartaches. Elvis confessed in 1962 that he *Can't Help Falling in Love*, while a decade later Harry Nilson's *Without You* contained the lines 'Can't live, if living is without you'. Counter-culturally, in 1971 Stephen Stills suggested we ought to *Love the One You're With*, while more recently Womack and Womack have sung about *Love Wars*, Rose Royce noticed that *Love Don't Live Here Anymore*, Freddie Mercury proclaimed that *Love Kills*, while Roxy Music suggested perceptively that *Love is the Drug*.

Romantic love developed as a system of belief, or ideology, in France during the last quarter of the twelfth century. Its theoretical basis was formulated by Andreus Capellanus in *The Art of Courtly Love*, and in the poetry of Chrêtien de Troyes. Carried to the countryside by troubadours, the idea of romantic love took hold and spread quite rapidly throughout Europe. Among the precepts and notions of courtly love were the following: the ennobling power of love; the conception of love as a burning, rarely extinguished, passion; the idea of fidelity between lovers, and, significantly, *the impossibility of love between husband and wife*. The thinking behind this is that love thrives on freedom of choice, is spontaneous and therefore not the fulfilment of a contract. Marriage, however, is a relationship with a fixed obligation; therefore marriage and love are incompatible. Other themes of courtly love dealt with nature, the naturalness of love affairs and the personification of love as a god.

Romanticism, as a movement, was similar to courtly love. The romanticist worshipped whatever was natural and characteristic of each individual. He cherished sensation and excitement, and considered that emotion was essential to life. Above all, the romanticist fueled his protest with youthful energy: Byron, Shelley, Keats, Wordsworth ('The good die first, And they whose hearts are dry as summer dust Burn to the socket'), Coleridge, Chateaubriand and Lamartine were all in their twenties and thirties when they made their major contributions. As with courtly love, romanticism could be 'mixed' in the sense that it fused the sensual and the pure – sexual love was the hieroglyph of divine love.

Modern culture considers romantic love to be *equivalent* to love. In other words, romantic love *is* love. Its characteristics, drawn from and developed out of courtly love and romanticism, include the notion of love at first sight: the importance of physical and emotional attraction; the belief that love conquers all; that women are more romantic than men; that love can be experienced as a sweeping, burning, rarely extinguished passion; the emphasis on fidelity (at least when still in love); the belief that love is constantly tinged with sadness – like parting, it is 'sweet sorrow'; and the conviction that for each person there is one predestined true love. Romantic love is the ideal of pure, unfulfilled love celebrated by the poets and enacted in so many of the great dramas – classic examples are the stories of Romeo and Juliet, Tristan and Iseult, Heloise and Abelard. And of course we all proclaim it to be 'beyond words', only to be experienced and not talked of, incapable of being measured. Well, I have a surprise for you, in the form of Zick Rubin, a psychologist from Harvard, who believes we *can* measure it.

Zick (to adopt familiar terms) starts from the assumption that romantic love may be 'independently conceptualised and measured'. He also assumes that 'love is an *attitude* held by a person toward a particular other person, involving predispositions to think, feel, and behave in certain ways toward that other person'. He continues this fog-like argument by 'defining' romantic love as 'love between unmarried opposite-sex peers, of the sort which could possibly lead to marriage'. Well yes, Zick. But what sort of love is this? How do such romantic lovers think, feel, behave, and act? Zick's reply is that romantic love includes three components: 'affiliative and dependent need, a predisposition to help, and an orientation of exclusiveness and absorption'. In other words: if I could never be with Mary I'd be miserable because I am so pathetic and so dependent on her; if Larry were feeling sick, my first duty would be to cheer him up – perhaps by cooking him his favourite lasagne; I feel extremely possessive about Jennifer and will kill you if you lay a finger on her, and I feel that I can tell her about everything (except the fact that I'm a transvestite).

Zick then develops a 'love-scale' as a way to distinguish between loving and liking. He gives questionnaires to dating couples and, depending on their scores, terms them strong-love couples or weak love couples. He reasons that as romantic love entails exclusiveness and absorption, he can safely 'predict' that in an 'unstructured laboratory situation, dating partners who loved each other a great deal would gaze into one another's eyes more than would partners who loved each other to a lesser degree'. So our intrepid experimenter goes further than man has been, enters the laboratory and measures the gazing couples. His prediction is confirmed: 'Couples who were strongly in love, as categorised by their scores on the love-scale, spent more time gazing into one another's eyes than did couples who were only weakly in love'. What an absolute surprise. But then Zick moves to the level of theory, announcing that his results are in accord with the assumption that 'gazing is a manifestation of the exclusive and absorptive component of romantic love'. Does this mean that blind people aren't in love? Can't we be in love without staring at each other? He concludes his monument to science with the observation that the lovers' estimates of the 'likelihood that they would marry their partners were more highly related to their love than to their liking for their partners'. And I always thought you married someone you disliked.

Incidentally Zick; in case you need to get in touch with me I've just moved.

The more serious and fruitful analyses of romantic love and its discontents have come from the more philosophically-minded psychologists such as Erich Fromm, Robert Johnson and M. Scott Peck. Fromm, in his now classic *The Art of Loving*, observes that people watch countless films about happy and unhappy love stories, listen to hundreds of 'trashy songs' about love – yet 'hardly anyone thinks there is anything that needs to be learned to love'. Fromm poses the question , 'Is love an art?' If so, it requires knowledge and effort. Or is love a pleasant sensation, a chance, something one 'falls into' if one is lucky? Fromm believes the former, although he considers that the majority of people today believe the latter. Consequently he sees three sets of problems. Firstly, most people regard love primarily in terms of being loved rather than of loving. Secondly, they assume that the problem of love is that of an object, not of a faculty. People think that to love is simple, but that to find the right object to love or to be loved by, is difficult. Fromm argues that because Western culture is based on the appetite for buying, on consumerism, on the idea of a mutually favourable exchange, so he, or she, looks at people in a similar way: 'For the man an attractive girl – and for a woman an attractive man – are the prizes they are after. "Attractive" usually means a nice package of qualities which are popular and sought after on the personality market.' He adds that what 'specifically makes a person attractive depends on the fashion of the time, physically as well as mentally'. Two people thus 'fall in love' when they feel they have found the best object available on the market, taking into account the limitations of their exchange values.

The third error lies in the confusion between the initial experience of 'falling' in love and the permanent state of 'being' in love, or as we might better put it, of 'standing' in love. Fromm argues that this 'miracle' of sudden intimacy is often facilitated if it is combined with, or initiated by, sexual attraction and consummation. However, this type of love, by its very nature, does not last. The two persons involved become well acquainted, but their intimacy slowly loses its miraculous character, until antagonism, disappointments and mutual boredom kill whatever is left of the initial excitement.

Fromm believes that the 'art of loving', like any other art, requires the mastery of both theory and practice; and he suggests why people in Western society so rarely endeavour to learn this art, given their obvious and painful failures: 'In spite of the deep-seated craving for love, almost everything else is considered to be more important than love: success, prestige, money, power – almost all our energy is used for the learning of how to achieve these aims, and almost none to learn the art of loving'.

Fromm describes and evaluates love – 'a capacity of the mature, productive character' – in relation to the particular culture of contemporary Western societies. He claims that 'no objective observer of our Western life can doubt that love – brotherly love, motherly love, and erotic love – is a relatively rare phenomenon, and that its place is taken by a number of forms of pseudo-love which are in reality so many forms of the disintegration of love'. Automatons cannot love; they can simply exchange their 'personality packages' and hope for a fair bargain. In this concept of love and marriage, the main emphasis is on finding a refuge from an otherwise unbearable sense of aloneness. Love provides such a haven. An alliance of two is formed against the world, and this egoism *à deux* is mistaken for love and intimacy.

M. Scott Peck's book *The Road Less Travelled* has become a worldwide best-seller. Subtitled 'a new psychology of love, traditional values and spiritual growth', its success indicates that there is an obsessive interest in the subject and that it is a book of its time, its culture, a true product of the new narcissism or the new mood. Unlike Zick Rubin, for example, Peck acknowledges at the outset that 'love is too large, too deep ever to be truly understood or measured or limited within the framework of words'. Yet he has a crack at it, and subsequently defines love as 'the will to extend one's self for the purpose of nurturing one's own or another's spiritual growth'. I find this unhelpful; it comes over as a kind of benign elitism. I object to those who happen to believe in the 'spiritual' dimension telling *us* that we should have some of it in order to be whole, or indeed to be in love.

However, Peck is clear and helpful on what love *isn't*. Like Fromm, he asserts that 'falling in love' is not love; so what is it? With honesty he replies 'I do not know', but adds that the 'sexual specificity of the phenomenon leads me to suspect that it is a genetically determined instinctual component of mating behaviour'. Peck continues with an attack on our genes – as if *they* had minds – by elaborating that 'falling in love is a trick that our genes pull on our otherwise perceptive mind to hoodwink or trap us into marriage'.

To serve so effectively as a marriage trap, the experience of falling in love must surely foster the illusion that it will last forever. Peck's explanation is worth repeating in full:

'This illusion is fostered in our culture by the commonly held myth of romantic love, which has its origins in our favourite childhood fairy tales, wherein the prince and princess, once united, live happily forever after. The myth of romantic love tells us, in effect, that for every young man in the world there is a young woman who was "meant for him", and vice versa. Moreover, the myth implies that there is only one man meant for a woman and only one woman for a man and this has been predetermined "in the stars". When we meet the person for whom we are intended, recognition comes through the fact that we fall in love. We have met the person for whom all the heavens intended us, and since the match is perfect, we will then be able to satisfy all of each other's needs forever and ever, and therefore live happily forever in perfect union and harmony.'

Of course, should we, God forbid, fall *out* of love, or fail to satisfy each other's needs, then it is 'clear that a dreadful mistake was made, we misread the stars, we did not hook up with our one and only perfect match, what we thought was love was not real or "true" love'. So nothing can be done about this except to get divorced – or to live unhappily for ever after. Unlike the fairy tales.

Peck, however, then turns the argument on its head by suggesting that 'falling in love' is in fact very, very close to 'real love'; so much so that the misconception that falling in love is true love is so potent *precisely* because it 'contains a grain of truth'. Falling in love, the subsequent temporary loss of self (of ego boundaries) and the activity of sexual intercourse not only lead us to make commitments to other people from which 'real love may begin', but in addition give us a hint of the more 'lasting mystical ecstasy that can be ours after a lifetime of love'. Peck then adds, helpfully if not originally, that the second most common misconception is the idea that dependency is love. He puts it in the following manner: 'When you require another individual for your survival, you are a parasite on that individual . . . there is no choice, no freedom involved in your relationship . . . it is a matter of necessity rather than love'. Two people love each other only when they are quite capable of living without each other but nonetheless choose to live with each other.

Peck has something in common with the author of another set of best-selling books, Robert A. Johnson, and his trilogy *He, She* and *We*. *We*, subtitled 'understanding the psychology of romantic love', is a Jungian interpretation of the myth of Tristan and Iseult. This myth, argues the author, not only records the dynamics of romantic love in 'the male psyche', but also reflects the fate of feminine values of feelings, relatedness and 'soul consciousness' which have been 'virtually driven out of our culture by our patriarchal mentality'. Another insight provided by the myth is the degree to which most men unconsciously search for 'their lost feminine side, for the feminine values in life, and an attempt to find their unlived feminine side through women'.

The myth of Tristan and Iseult portrays the life of young Tristan who grows into a noble and selfless hero and then encounters the overwhelming experience in his life, his passion for Queen Iseult. Johnson claims that the myth vividly symbolises the development of a male consciousness as Tristan struggles to win his masculinity, to become aware, too, of his feminine side and to deal with love and responsibility. It shows a man torn by the conflicting forces and loyalties that rage within the male psyche when he is consumed by the joys, passions and sufferings of romance.

More generally, Johnson claims that myths give us 'specific psychological information' and teach us the 'deep truths of the psyche'. The trouble with this argument, though, is that he fails to recognise a myth as a social product, *created* by particular people at a particular time. It is, in other words, a specific *cultural* product. His universalistic interpretation is interesting and to some extent valid; but it fits his psychological theory too neatly. He does not so much discover truth in the myth as impose meaning on it. Indeed, he rather contradicts himself in wanting to stress the universalistic psychological truths of romantic love yet also to emphasise that this love is a Western phenomenon (we are accustomed to think of it as the only form of love), pointing to the fact that Eastern cultures do not impose such impossible demands.

Employing the Jungian jargon of *anima*, the man's feminine side, and *animus*, the woman's masculine side, Johnson claims that within the individual these have to be carefully balanced. He argues that the 'strongest man is the one who can genuinely show love to his children, as well as fight his battles in the business world during the work day . . . his masculine strength is augmented and balanced by his feminine capacity to be related, to express his affection and his feelings'. Trying to slip the noose of sexism, he adds that each of us must develop both sides of the psyche. We must be able to handle power and to develop the capacity to love, to exert control and to 'flow spontaneously with fate'. The problem, in his view, is that we have not begun to realise this potential; we have so far taken the wrong turning.

> 'Western people are children of inner poverty, though outwardly we have everything. Probably no other people in history have been so lonely, so alienated, so confused over values, so neurotic. We have dominated our environment with sledgehammer force and electronic precision. We amass riches on an unprecedented scale. But few of us, very few indeed, are at peace with ourselves, secure in our relationships, content in our loves, or at home in the world. Most of us cry out for meaning in life, for values we can live by, for love and relationships.'

The source of such troubles is romantic love which, he claims, is the single greatest energy system in the Western psyche, and which has supplanted religion as the arena in which men and women seek meaning, transcendence, wholeness and ecstasy. Johnson adds, in a vein similar to Fromm and Peck, that romantic love certainly isn't real love, but rather a psychological phenomenon with very specific characteristics. Romantic love doesn't just mean loving someone, it also means 'being in love'. In this state we believe we have found the ultimate meaning in life, revealed in another human being. We have discovered the bits missing from ourselves and now begin to feel whole. This psychological package includes the unconscious demand that our lover should *always* provide us with such feelings of ecstasy and intensity. The trouble is that with the onset of feelings of loneliness or frustration at our inability to make genuinely long and committed relationships, we blame the other for failing us: 'It doesn't occcur to us that perhaps it is we who need to change our own unconscious attitudes' and 'the expectations and demands we impose on our relationships and on other people'.

Johnson believes, with Peck, that if we realised that romantic love, being in love, was merely a beginning, a potentiality, and not love itself, we might salvage something from its often disastrous effects. Falling in love, he argues, is not something that one controls, rather it happens *to* you, and so long as we're 'in love' with someone the world takes on a brightness and meaningfulness that no mortal human being *in fact* could ever bestow. But when we fall 'out of love' the world suddenly seems dismal and empty, even though we are still with the same human being who formerly inspired such rapture. This is why men and women put such impossible demands on each other in their relationships: 'We actually believe unconsciously that this mortal human being has the responsibility for making our lives whole, keeping us happy, making our lives meaningful, intense, and ecstatic.'

This illusion, originating in courtly love and fostered by Romanticism, has gradually affected the values by which we live. Romance, with its singular aim of passion, has taken over our lives. Everything else – obligation, duty, relationship, commitment – is secondary. Johnson claims that from the twelfth century onward we began to believe that the most important thing in life is to search for 'one's soul through romantic projection' and that 'we have not learned that there is any other way to find our soul'. This ideal of romance teaches us that we must seek the ultimate ecstasy, discover the 'enchanted orchard', by the one means known to us – falling in love. We believe we have the right to pursue passion no matter who we hurt, regardless of any relationship we may damage *en route*. Johnson believes that real love is a feeling directed at another human being, not an expression of personal passion, and that love desires the well-being and happiness of one's beloved, not a great drama at the other's expense. As he says, it does not occur to Western people 'that a relationship could be made between two ordinary mortal human beings, that they could love each other as ordinary imperfect people and could simply allow the projections to evaporate'. Indeed, the only enduring relationships will be between couples who 'consent to see each other as ordinary, imperfect people and who love each other without illusion and without inflated expectations'. He continues:

'One of the great paradoxes in romantic love is that *it never produces human relationships as long as it stays romantic*. It produces drama, daring adventure, wondrous, intense love scenes, jealousies and betrayals; but people never seem to settle into relationships with each other as flesh-and-blood human beings until

51

they're out of the romantic love state, until they *love* each other instead of "being in love".'

The message, therefore, is relatively simple. Romantic love is a psychological state which takes on a life of its own, and which, as fantasy, has relatively little to do with the person we have fallen 'in love' with. Only when we learn to know ourselves and others, only when we understand that romantic love is an illusion, will real love begin to develop. This real love is more 'spiritual' than psychological. Wise people, of course, have been saying this for a long time, but Johnson is to be congratulated for resurrecting the idea. There are, nonetheless, problems with his account.

For a start, he works with a model of us – you and me – which although flattering is not necessarily realistic. Not all of us *desire* the deepness, the authenticity, the wholeness, the love that he so eloquently describes. Some of us *cannot* have it. People are so very diferent. They have different occupations: zoo keepers, bank managers, drillers, teachers, musicians, wage-slaves, cameramen, shop assistants. Different personalities: moody, mean, aggressive, intuitive, angry, placid. Different values: individualistic, communal, fascist, accommodating. Different degrees of sexuality: obsessed mentally and physically, generous, relatively frigid. And as to the attainment of self-knowledge and knowledge of others, many of us, if we searched deeply inside ourselves, wouldn't find a lot. It is only an assumption that within us, at a subterranean level, there is a 'real self' which can be located and excavated through self-knowledge. Some of us live life simply, maybe too simply. We play psychological games, nurse secrets, practise deceits. We men may be aware of a feminine psyche, expressed perhaps in a parental role and through occasional bouts of tenderness. We may even cry. And the male psyche will surface when we seek power and status at work. But most of the time we are in a daze – products of our childhood, of choice, of culture, of other people, of delusion. So the search for self-knowledge is much harder than Johnson suggests. Besides, most of us neither have the time nor resources, let alone the inclination, for psychotherapy. And what do you do when you ultimately 'find yourself' and dislike the picture that emerges? As for knowledge of others, again we're in the arena of self-presentation and identity management, with all the veils that surround such processes. In any event, does the 'other' know *herself*? And so it goes on.

Ironically, Johnson underestimates the strength and power of romantic love, the *cultural* forces that keep it in operation and the subsequent struggle, usually unsuccessful, of changing our spots. I have had unhappy relationships, made other people suffer. But have I learnt? My psychology (and my friends) say no. Am I that unusual? I think not.

If romantic love conceals more truths than it reveals, so does its *alter ego*, loneliness. The nature of the relationship between romantic love and loneliness is perfectly described by Frank Elliot, the tortured central character of Ted Whitehead's play *Alpha Beta*: 'O.K . . . we're both trapped. (*Pause*). You know, it's crazy . . . Society is organised to create loneliness . . . the loneliness that leads to marriage. Society creates the disease . . . then prescribes a worse one as cure. Men enslave women . . . then wake up to find they've enslaved themselves!'

Heartache and loneliness

Jimmy Ruffin sung 'What becomes of the broken hearted?' while Phil Collins pleaded 'Don't let him steal your heart away'. In 1965 Tony Bennett left his heart in San Francisco; so it's not surprising that we have heard so little of him lately. An anthropologist friend of mine, renowned for his ability to 'know' so many women, usually one after the other but often simultaneously, is nicknamed 'heartbreaker'. What does this imagery mean? Why should a four-chambered double pump, situated between the lungs somewhat left of centre, behind the breastbone, resting on the diaphragm, weighing 8-12 ounces, depending on gender, have any connection with either the gaining or losing of love? Songs such as 'I left my brain in San Francisco', or 'Don't let him steal your brain away' would sound a bit odd. But why the imagery of the heart? The quick answer is because when we meet someone to whom we are extremely attracted, our heartbeat goes bananas; and when the other person eventually realises we aren't worth knowing, it slows down and aches, or races and stops. But does it?

Numerous examples, as well as intuition, appear to support the contention of researcher James Lynch that the 'lack of human companionship, the sudden loss of love, and chronic human loneliness are significant contributors to serious desease (including cardiovascular disease) and premature death'. In *The Broken Heart: The Medical Consequences of Loneliness*, he distinguishes between those factors that *predispose* an individual to diseases such as cardiovascular disease, and factors that *precipitate* immediate heart changes, some of which can lead to sudden death. Lynch provides many examples of sudden deaths caused by 'emotional factors':

'A 52-year-old man had been in close contact with his physician during his wife's terminal illness with lung cancer. Examination, including electrocardiogram, 6 months before her death, showed no evidence of coronary disease. He died suddenly of a massive myocardial infarction the day after his wife's funeral'.

'A 40-year-old father slumped dead as he cushioned the head of his son lying injured in the street beside his motorcycle'.

'A 17-year-old boy collapsed and died at 6. a.m., June 4, 1970; his older brother had died at 5.12 a.m., June 4, 1969, of multiple injuries incurred in an auto accident several hours earlier. The cause of the younger boy's death was massive sub-arachnoid hemorrhage caused by a ruptured anterior communicating artery aneurysm'.

'A 55-year-old man died when he met his 88-year-old father after a 20-year separation; the father then dropped dead'.

'A 90-year-old man died 6 hours after his wife came home from the hospital, presumably recovered from a heart attack. She herself then had another attack and died 13 hours later'.

It is not just bereavement that can cause so much harm. Lynch argues, on the basis of mortality statistics, that for all ages, for both sexes, and for all races in the USA, the non-married always have higher death rates, sometimes as much as five times higher than those of married individuals. (And we all know that unpleasantness *within* marriage and the family doesn't help our mental or physical health either.) He concentrates on the disruption of human relationships that has occurred in the USA as a result of the rapidly increasing divorce rate. Of course, severe life changes such as divorcing or being divorced, or being the child of divorced parents, creates emotional stress. Like Lasch and Sennett, Lynch asserts that recent changes which stress independence and individualism, but denigrate dependency, simply do not help us. In our contemporary societies, 'to need someone else is viewed as a sign of weakness, a social sin'. And unlike Peck and Johnson, Lynch believes that the new social moods of independence make it 'increasingly difficult to share the most basic of all human truths: that people desperately need each other, that we really are dependent on one another'. Because of feelings of 'shame', we too often deceive ourselves and claim that we are neither lonely nor need companionship. Conversely, we panic and attempt to find a companion too quickly, too eagerly. And because we are driven by romantic love, we often, or indeed invariably, choose inadequately and create even more problems for ourselves, increased loneliness rather than less. In conclusion, Lynch argues that men who jog to keep their 'hearts in shape' apparently see little connection between the 'shape' of their marriages, the 'shape' of their general social milieu, and the 'shape' of their hearts. Well, I do. One of the reasons I don't jog is because I'm always worn out after family arguments and feel unable to reach for the Reeboks.

To be serious. I am, for argument's sake, a Martian, and what I see from my world is this. Best-sellers Peck and Johnson say that dependency on someone else is not love, that two people love each other only when they are quite capable of living without each other, but nonetheless choose to live with each other. Lynch, however, tells me that human dialogue is the elixir of life, and that the ultimate decision is simple – we must live together or increase our chances of unhappiness, ill health and the big sleep. And he stresses the need for dependency in our relationships. Here on Mars, however, we have no such problems. We have relationships that are satisfying, we like being together *and* apart, and when one partner dies we cry and then rejoice as they go to a 'better place' and in any case we're allowed to find a replacement straight away. No big deal. There are no such things here as dependency, lifelong commitment and coupledom: you only *feel* what you are taught to *think*.

You can see my point. Modern Western societies *do* stress

coupledom, almost to the point of belief that people who do not couple-up are mad; indeed, psychiatrist Irving Bieber asserts that there is 'increasing recognition that bachelorhood is symptomatic of psychopathology'.

With this sort of pressure, it is not surprising to find evidence of the negative consequences of social isolation or of the failure to form emotional attachments. In his study of self-destructive behaviours, more plainly entitled *Pathways to Suicide*, (1981), Ronald W. Maris points to the fact that social isolation and emotional deprivation can lead to undesirable and painful states, as evidenced in the reactions to 'wintering over' in the Antarctic.

The problems related to the individual's adjustment to close group interdependence, monotony of environment, and absence of accustomed sources of emotional gratification were studied among groups of volunteers subjected to Antarctic living for periods of six to eight months at isolated US bases. Scientists, officers and enlisted personnel lived in groups of 12 to 40; each man was assigned a specific job and hence was dependent on every other man. Technical competence, responsibility and stability in job performance thus became key factors in determining group acceptance and status. Maris argues that reactions such as those cited below are of special interest in terms of their possible relevance to similar conditions in space travel.

Symptoms observed

Intellectual inertia	Lack of energy for intellectual pursuits, especially during winter. Earlier plans to catch up on reading or learn a foreign language are rarely realised.
Impaired memory and concentration	Varied from absent-mindedness and poor concentration to marked lowering of intellectual acuity and periods of amnesia. Most pronounced during winter months.
Insomnia	Varying degrees of sleeplessness, again mostly in winter. Individual felt tired but unable to relax.
Headaches	Frequent headaches, more common

	among the officer-scientist group than among the enlisted men. Appeared to be of psychogenic origin and possibly related to repression and control of hostility.
Hostility	Relatively little overt hostility expressed, probably because of the tremendous need for relatedness and group acceptance in these small, isolated groups. Social censure, in the form of the 'silent treatment', inflicted on the occasional troublesome individual resulted in 'long-eye' syndrome – varying degrees of sleeplessness, crying, hallucinations, deterioration in personal hygiene, and a tendency to move aimlessly about or to lie in bed staring blankly into space until again accepted by group.
Depression	Low-grade depression prevalent, particularly during winter months. Of six men who became psychiatric casualties, three diagnosed as cases of relatively severe neurotic depression.
Appetite	Appetite for food greatly increased, possibly because of absence of other gratifications. Weight gains of 20 to 30 pounds not unusual.

Among Maris's many conclusions is that 'suicide completers' are more socially isolated than non-fatal suicide attempters or indeed those who die natural deaths. Moreover, in the year previous to a suicide attempt or actual death, suicide completers have fewer close friends and are more likely either to be divorced or never to have married. Let us now turn, however, to the systematic study of enforced human solitude, *loneliness*, in an attempt to answer the

57

question of whether we do really need others for survival.

The world of fiction has, of course, explored loneliness as a central predicament in human drama. Defoe's *Robinson Crusoe*, George Eliot's *Silas Marner*, Bronte's *Wuthering Heights*, Hesse's *Steppenwolf*, Thomas Wolfe's *Look Homeward Angel* and Hemingway's *The Old Man and the Sea* are but a few examples. Suzanne Gordon in her *Lonely in America* (1976) argues that loneliness, once a philosophical problem, 'spoken of mainly by poets and prophets, has now become an almost permanent condition for millions of Americans', and that 'knowing no limits of class, race, or age, loneliness today is a great leveller, a new American tradition'. It is a human emotion 'common to all people in all eras', but at certain points in history, through specific social changes, what were 'inevitable moments in life' become, sometimes overnight, lifestyles for millions of people – changes such as increased geographical mobility, death of a loved one and divorce on an unprecedented scale. So what *is* loneliness? How may we describe it or characterise it?

We all know roughly what the term indicates, but may not be able to conceptualise it as precisely, say, as academics from Los Angeles who have spent decades investigating the condition and developing scales in an attempt to 'measure' it. Nevertheless, *our* opinions are the important ones – because each of us has our own unique experience of it. How can it ever be measured? Indeed, how much is too much; or, more importantly, how little loneliness is bearable? Just as we all experience falling in love differently, we all experience loneliness differently. So what can we really know about it?

Suzanne Gordon suggests that loneliness seems to 'universally indicate the following major components': feelings of hopelessness, which lead people to escape into relationships that may appear solidly grounded but are really only a means to another end, not an end in itself: fear of actually experiencing such feelings of loneliness; the desire to deny that we are in fact lonely; and feelings of worthlessness and failure because of our experience of loneliness. Robert S. Weiss, in his most valuable analysis of the subject, observes that the desire for company, and notably a special kind of relationship, is the major characteristic of loneliness. As he puts it, the responsiveness of loneliness to the right sort of relationship is remarkable – given the establishment of such a relationship, 'loneliness' will vanish abruptly and without trace, as though it has never existed: 'There is no gradual recovery, or getting over it bit by bit . . . when it ends, it ends suddenly; one was lonely, one is not any more.' Weiss then makes the most important distinction between the experience of loneliness and that of depression. In loneliness there is a drive to rid oneself of the feelings of distress by initiating a new relationship or regaining a lost one, but in depression there is a surrender to the distress. The lonely, in other words, have the urge to find others, and if these are the right ones, they change and no longer feel lonely. The depressed, on the other hand, are often unwilling to impose their unhappiness on others, and their feelings, in any case, are often unaffected by relationships, old *or* new.

Our feelings, thoughts and sensations, when lonely, vary not only from individual to individual, but also in strength. We may look pale, dejected and hopeless. We can have physical sensations of sickness and cold. We feel sad, uncertain, misunderstood, frightened and aimless. We miss having people around us with whom we can share joy or sorrow. We feel inner emptiness and a conviction that there is no cure to this hopeless situation unless we quickly find a mate. We accept that people are by nature unwilling to rescue us from our loneliness, that we are left to our own fate. In the USA there are over 16 million persons living alone – equivalent to over 21 per cent of all American households – whether as a consequence of deliberate choice, divorce or death. In Britain, the statistics of widowhood are quite overwhelming. One woman in seven, and one woman in two over the age of 65, is a widow; and *daily* 500 wives become widows. But not all of these people are necessarily lonely, so that we have to make two sets of important distinctions if we are to hack our way through the conceptual jungle of academic literature.

Firstly, Jenny de Jong-Gierveld and Jos Raad Schelders note that in philosophical discussions there has been a distinction between *positive* and *negative* experiences of what German philosophers have termed *einsamkeit*. In positive terms this experience is akin to solitude – an opportunity for reflection and self-communication, a means of testing strength of character by choosing to spend time alone. The negative aspects of *einsamkeit*, sometimes called *vereinsamung*, are

59

nearer to our concept of loneliness. Inwardly the individual can experience an estrangement from the self and from others, a feeling of alienation even in company. External cicumstances such as the death of a partner or the loss of friends can also lead to negative feelings of loneliness. The second construct allows us, therefore, to build on the earlier distinction. Fundamentally it is helpful to distinguish between psychological and societal explanations of loneliness.

The psychology of loneliness

The psychological approaches to loneliness vary quite considerably. Possibly the first psychological analysis of loneliness was by Zilboorg (1938) who believed that loneliness was a reflection of narcissism, of megalomania. Such a person retains infantile feelings of omnipotence, and is egocentric. Loneliness therefore originates in the crib. The helpless infant learns the joys of being loved and admired, as well as the shock of being weak and having to depend on others. This period of infantile experience is the quintessence of what becomes a narcissistic orientation. The great psychoanalyst Harry Stack Sullivan also saw the roots of adult loneliness in childhood. For him the driving need for human intimacy first appears in the child's need for contact, followed by the adolescent's craving for friends. Those who lack the necessary social skills because of damaged relationships with parents subsequently have difficulties forming friendships, and this inability may well develop into full-blown loneliness. Another psychoanalyst, Frieda Fromm-Reichman, indeed believes that such loneliness may show in, or ultimately lead to, 'the development of psychotic states'. While Robert Weiss supports the views of British psychiatrist John Bowlby, and argues that as loneliness is 'allayed only by the relationship in which there is assurance of the continued accessibility of someone trusted', it is clear that the absence of attachments is the cause of the form of loneliness he calls 'emotional isolation'. Bowlby believes that just as monkeys can wither away and pine to death through the loss of attachments, so we humans too need emotional attachments to sustain a meaningful life.

The humanist-cum-phenomenological approach of Carl Rogers argues that the social pressures which envelop the individual may often propel that particular person to act in a manner which could well

Elvis in *Jailhouse Rock* – life has never been the same since. *(Rex Features)*

Are we humans really like other animals? *(Fotofolio/ Inge Morath)*

Do animals fall in love?

Perhaps we *are* like our nearest relatives, the apes.

Perfect partners?

A sixties radical is mourned in *The Big Chill*. *(Colombia Pictures)*

Perfect partners?

Above Loneliness
or solitude?

Perfect partners?

lead to a discrepancy between his inner self and the self presented to others. Loneliness thus occurs when such individuals drop their defences to reveal themselves but nevertheless anticipate or experience rejection from others. Rogers does not emphasise the role of childhood; for him loneliness is an ongoing problem of self, true self, and society. The psychological approach also stresses the role of perception or cognition in the production of an experience of loneliness. This occurs when an individual *perceives* a discrepancy between desired and actual achieved level of social contact. Such needs and desires obviously vary. The expectations of some individuals are excessively high, others perhaps exceedingly low. Sadler and Johnson make the same point in distinguishing between isolation and loneliness. For them the meaning of isolation depends on how a person interprets his situation. In contrast to isolated existence, which appears to be an adaptive, external condition, loneliness is an experience which is subjective and internal. Isolation *may* contribute to loneliness but cannot simply be reduced to it.

Joseph Hartog makes a similar point by arguing that the impact of individual loneliness depends on whether or not such solitude has *meaning*. Meaningless or self-depreciating loneliness is of a very different order from that loneliness which has an understandable cause or which results from an act of will. Highly motivated hermits, martyrs, scientists, artists, explorers, *usually* handle loneliness better than the abandoned, deserted, widowed or divorced because their experience has more meaning.

Finally, there is the approach of the existentialists who claim, quite correctly, that we are all ultimately alone, that no one can actually experience our feelings and thoughts, and that separateness is an essential condition of our existence. It is simply our destiny both to be alone and aware of it. Paul Tillich, the Lutheran theologian, observes that in the Eden story we read that 'then the Lord God said "It is not good that man should be alone"', so He creates woman from the body of Adam. Myth, he asserts, shows that there was originally no separation between man and woman. In the beginning they were one; now they are longing to be one again.

'But, although they recognise each other, and, although longing for each other, they see their strangeness . . . They are alone. The creation of the woman has not conquered the situation which God describes as not good for man. He remains alone, and the creation of the woman, although providing a helper for Adam, has only added to the one human being who is alone another human being who is equally alone, and out of them all the others, each of whom is also alone'.

One of the leading exponents of the existentialist approach, Clark E. Moustakas, makes what he believes to be an important distinction between 'true loneliness' and what he terms 'loneliness anxiety', which is in essence a defence mechanism that distracts individuals from dealing with crucial questions and motivates them instead to seek activity – often fruitless or frivolous – with others. True loneliness, on the other hand, stems from the reality of being alone and consequently facing life's ultimate experiences alone. Far from being a crippling, depressing condition, true loneliness is *potentially* an experience 'of being human which enables the individual to sustain, extend and deepen his humanity'. Moustakas adds that 'man's inevitable and infinite loneliness is not soley an awful condition of human existence' but also the 'instrument through which man experiences new compassion and new beauty'. This perspective is the same box of tricks which Peck and Johnson opened with their spiritual definition of 'love'. Moustakas relates the example of Antoine De Saint-Exupéry, author of *Wind, Sand and Stars, Night Flight, Flight to Arras* and *The Little Prince*, who, lost in the desert, endangered, naked between sand and sky, and enveloped in silence, then realised the full meaning of loneliness. During these days and nights, Saint-Exupéry came to understand himself and the nature of man; although awareness of these realities often did not strike home until later, he knew that 'in loneliness an essential inner need is satisfied and that no external power can ever prevail against self-fulfilment'. We will return to this in a moment.

The sociology of loneliness

The essential point is the awful reality of the *life-cycle*. We cannot escape age, and as we face middle-age, old-age, even senility, there is

62

the increasing likelihood that we will experience loss of partners, deprivation of social contracts, networks or communities. Claude Fischer and Susan Phillips argue that for men, ageing increases the risk of isolation, partly because of the decreased mobility and the death of friends. Marriage, however, protects them against kin isolation, and provides at least one confidant. Ageing has less impact on women, but marriage has more effect: it tends to isolate women from non-kin. There are many other obvious sociological examples of social and cultural changes which inevitably isolate people and increase their vulnerability to feelings of loneliness. They include social and geographical mobility; the trend toward smaller families and hence fewer kin; the isolating effects of modern architecture; changing attitudes towards the division of labour (feelings of isolation may be experienced by children of working mothers and by mothers who are prevented from working); and shifting cultural moods and expectations, which may encourage some individuals to crave independence yet inadvertently experience isolation, or, conversely, proclaim that to be surrounded by people is normal and that to be lonely is to be a failure. Finally, and most importantly, there is the *ideology of romantic love*, the throbbing message which tells us that if we do not 'fall in love', be part of a couple, constantly and forever, we are essentially deviant. No wonder so many of us feel so very lonely.

What can we learn from this gallop through the history of ideas? Three lessons, I believe. In the first place, loneliness, viewed either negatively or positively, is nonetheless awful. It is painful, claustrophobically private yet shameful, and seemingly unending. Secondly, although it is true that each of us, ultimately, is alone and that dipping into the depths of this 'true loneliness' can provide valuble self-knowledge, it is misleading and unhelpful to claim this as some form of heroism. When Clark Moustakas argues that the poet Emily Dickinson lived alone in almost complete isolation for a quarter of a century, and yet that much of her poetry was inspired by 'this intimate, monastic attachment', a force that continued to give 'direction to her productive capabilities for the rest of her life', he is not talking about you and me. Few of us practise creative monasticism. Besides, Moustakas tends to equate the solitude necessary, say, for artistic creation with loneliness. The notion that the artist retires from

63

the world to compose, to write, to paint, and that the 'creative process' must therefore involve loneliness, is actually a myth. Quite the contrary. It is essentially positive and productive, it is about hope and promise, and fundamentally it has meaning.

Finally, I believe that the majority of us are lonely most of the time. Our heads are not full of existential dilemmas and conundrums but rather of ideologies, like the necessity of romantic love, which itself creates expectations that cannot be realised. In and out of relationships, in and out of marriage, in the single or bereaved state, our desires are too often unrealistic, although some of us, of course, are lucky. But one of the central features of our culture is the frantic and terrifying fear of being alone – of not being part of a couple. As Suzanne Gordon puts it, the association between 'failure, loneliness, and solitude is so strong in our culture that people often find it difficult to believe that there are some who like being by themselves'.

If we are to rescue ourselves and our children from such an illusion, we must learn to throw off the shackles of romantic love, not in order to peak full of spiritual love (whatever that really means), but so that we may begin to discover who other people really are, find ourselves, and have relationships which are based on reality and not fantasy. Part of the process necessary for this transformation of culture – for that is what it amounts to – is the acceptance of solitude as a right in itself, and as a means to the end of self-knowledge. This is not easy.

I am not proposing that we become hermits or closet existentialists, or indeed that we should overvalue the experience of solitude. Rather that we give ourselves *real* time to think, find and feel. May Sarton, in her honest and moving *Journal of a Solitude*, offers a quartet of insights which summarise poetically my own conclusions:

> 'The value of solitude – one of its values – is, of course, that there is nothing to *cushion* against attacks from within, just as there is nothing to help balance at times of particular stress or depression . . . '
> 'If we are to understand the human condition, and if we are to accept ourselves in all the complexity, self-doubt, extravagance of feeling, guilt, joy, the slow freeing of the self to its full capacity for action and creation, both as human being and as

artist, we have to know all we can about each other, and we have to be willing to go naked . . . '

And quoting Louis Lavelle's *Le Mal et la Souffrance*,

'We sense that there can be no true communion between human beings until they have in fact become beings: for to be able to give oneself one must have taken possession of oneself in that painful solitude outside of which nothing belongs to us and we have nothing to give . . . '

For her there is 'only one real deprivation', and that is 'not to be able to give one's gifts to those one loves most'.

4

From hope to 'Heartbreak Hotel' in five easy lessons

'I've just been introduced to the New Maths, which is horrific for me because maths courses are the ones I failed at school. I can't quite figure out these new equations.

A forty-year-old doctor facilitated my introduction by telling me at a party that he only dated women in their mid-to-late twenties.

"Let me get this straight," I said, balancing a drink and a hefty serving of pâté, "I'm a decade younger than you are, but hypothetically I'm already too old for you. Right?"

"There's nothing hypothetical about it," he grinned, pâté glistening on his tie. "You *are* too old for me".'

Jean Gonick

For complex historical and cultural reasons, each generation has a set of stereotypes representing the perfect partner. Some of us are lucky; some of us *do* possess knowledge both of ourselves and our partners; some of us have learned, often painfully, of what lies behind the surface. But most of us haven't. The dream, the fantasy, is sold both to men and women. Both sexes cherish a mental image of the model partner.

Other forces, of course, are at work in this area of attraction. Some clearly go back to childhood. A woman's recollection of her relationship with her father is likely to have some bearing on her later choice of a mate. And if my reading of Freud is correct, we men continually search for a mother, a representation of *our* mother, to the end of time. Although, of course, when our unconscious remembers how our mummy let us down at times, we search for the opposite.

Even so, it is modern advertising more than anything else that has assisted us in our determination to delude ourselves, which is something we never tire of doing. Occasionally we may feel that we overestimate its influence; if so, we're quite wrong. 'Promise', noted Samuel Johnson in the eighteenth century, 'is the soul of advertisement.' Well, things haven't changed. Advertising *is* a promise, a technique for making us believe that life can be different, an instrument for filling us with hope – a hope that often has no possibility of fulfilment. The influence of advertising cannot be measured simply in terms of whether or not I go to my local shop and buy a packet of striped condoms after I've seen a celebrity demonstrate their use on television. Rather, it has to be assessed over a long period and in terms of how it has affected our vocabulary of life, the cultural air we breathe. This it certainly *has* done. As Christopher Lasch puts it in *The Culture of Narcissism*, advertising serves not so much to advertise products as to 'promote consumption as a way of life'. It upholds consumption as the answer to the age-old discontents of loneliness, sickness, weariness and lack of sexual satisfaction; and, he adds, 'at the same time it create new forms of discontent peculiar to the modern age'. Consumption promises to fill the aching void, 'hence the attempt to surround commodities with an aura of romance; with allusions to exotic places and vivid experiences; and with images of female breasts from which all blessings flow'. In fact, we speak to one another by courtesy of advertising symbols and images. The version of truth demonstrated and proposed by advertising clouds our view. It is the modern state's official art.

To be honest, something I am not too keen on doing, over the years I've met tall women, thin women, blondes, mods, high-fashion women, smart women, sexy women – but I've very rarely met *them* as people. In other words I've been duped, and still am very often. My head has always been full of images of the kinds of women I *ought* to know. In fact as a narcissistic, plump, depressing sort of bloke I

67

should really have met quite different kinds of women – but it has always been too late.

Pornography is the theory and rape is the practice

I intend to concentrate on advetising's images of women because, inevitably, in a patriarchal society women rather than men will be more unrealistically portrayed or symbolically exploited. Any form of sexist advertising is totally unacceptable, and in the case of women it represents symbolic annihilation.

> 'I am alone in the underground waiting for a train. All around me are huge images of female parts; giant rubbery peach tone breasts, wet lips, denim bums, damp looking stomachs, long legs in high heels . . . I don't know where to look that doesn't make me feel vulnerable or angry. A man comes into the tunnel and looks me up and down. All these ads are like his gang . . . '

Much print advertising *is* pornographic, in the sense that it explicitly describes or exhibits sexual activity intended to stimulate erotic as opposed to aesthetic feelings. Sexist advertising continues to be developed, though, in a multitude of shapes and forms in different media, and with only minimal opposition within the industry itself. John Downing, in *The Media Machine*, clearly oversimplifies the point when he conceptualises the relationship between women and their advertising image *solely* as the 'twentieth century shrinkage of women to vagina-on-legs', but he does have a point.

The two major areas of distorted representations of women in ads are firstly where women (and occasionally men) are portrayed solely as sex objects, and secondly where women are portrayed in *dependent roles*, except in the arenas of motherhood and the kitchen. As Jane Root ironically notes in *Pictures of Women*, women are often made 'absurdly ecstatic by very simple products, as though a new brand of floor cleaner or deodorant really could make all the difference to a lifetime'. Television personalities and celebrities are often recruited to show housewives how to use appliances, and white-coated scientists are brought in to instruct women migraine sufferers how to take a pill. In other advertisements, however, *men* are shown as totally unable to cope, incapable even of giving themselves a spoonful of cough medicine. Root adds that the 'majority of women who appear in advertisements are distinguished by their youth and beauty'; they are the 'girlfriends' who appear alongside their men in shampoo and chocolate advertisements, and the sensuous 'models' and *femmes fatales* who act as status symbols, offering accessories to successful men. Other sexy women, often scantily clad, can be seen sprawled over car bonnets, or enticingly wrapped around stereos.

Advertising makes a woman 'nothing more than the commodities she wears: the lipstick, the tights, the clothes and so on are "woman"', argues Janice Winship, in *Sexuality for Sale*. Advertising, especially in print, certainly lends enormous vitality to the idea that the female body must be fully acceptable to its actual or potential male users, and so women are systematically pressured to accept being reduced to a 'body-for-men', and even pay generously for the privilege. From childhood, women are conditioned to be more concerned with their faces and bodies in order to please men with their appearance and looks. As Estée Lauder puts it: 'People have said that my products are too expensive, but they're the people who don't understand that real security is only achieved by feeling beautiful.' They are led to believe that being beautiful and making the most of their 'femininity' will invariably lead to certain rewards.

As a subplot of this theme, women are prodded to compete with each other for the scarce resource named 'man'. Never far from the surface in advertising is the presumption that even the woman attached to one man must be careful to 'keep' him, or better bodies may entice him away. Question: as for unattached women, how are they to end their predicament satisfactorily? Answer: by riveting the attention of the man they want, and not choking him with body odour or disgusting him with carelessly trimmed cuticles. In soap advertisements, for example, efficiency in promoting cleanliness is hardly ever the message, rather it is the soap's potential for *romance*, or for averting romantic disaster which is its key property.

Betty Friedan, in her classic *The Feminine Mystique* (1965), concluded her analysis of the advertising content of women's magazines by observing that manufacturers aimed to boost consumption of home products by reinforcing and rewarding the concept of woman's total fulfilment through the role of housewife and mother. Since then very little has changed. We only have to look at the evidence of our own eyes. Food, for example, is an interesting case of sexual stereo-typing, notably in relation to slimming. The message of most manu-facturers is that almost every girl and woman in the Western world should be worrying about her weight. In 1983, for instance, Kellogg's *Special K* 'thinking woman's diet' advertisement suggested that the 'thinking woman' should be concerned about her weight if she could 'pinch more than an inch'. Essentially, advertisers attempt to ensure either that women are not going to eat – 'Sorry, I can't, I'm slimming' – or, if they *do* eat, that it's 'naughty but nice', done secretly in the dark or one day in seven. Modern patriarchal Western societies value emaciation and physical immaturity, defining it as feminine beauty. These values, over which women have relatively little control, cause most women to be extremely anxious about food; and this anxiety is seized upon and exploited relentlessly by advertisers. Food is also the symbolic representation of the woman's role as nurturer, as provider *and* preparer of food for husband, family and friends. And there are even more pernicious themes, whereby women are represented virtually in terms of some appetising form of food.

Sexist advertising is offensive because it neither portrays women realistically nor helps them to develop confident self-images. It ought to be eliminated, yet it continues unabated, even though, addition-ally, it has been shown to be less effective than non-sexist advertising in terms of persuading the consumer to purchase. As Alexander and Judd put it – in an article noted more for its title than its content, *Do Nudes in Ads Enhance Brand Recall?* – 'While an illustration of a nude female may gain the interest and attention of a viewer, an advertise-ment depicting a nonsexual scene appears to be more effective in obtaining brand recall.'

Advertising, in tandem with the ideology of romantic love, creates an environment which not only produces some rather strange cases of mate selection but also provides a painful reminder of our inability to match unrealistic expectations. In my view, sex has taken over practically every aspect of our lives. And few of us are immune to sexual pressure in one form or another. This can range from young girls who confide in their friend and ask 'How far should I go?' to the 'new man' who neurotically and repeatedly askes 'Was it good for you?' as he casually checks his performance time on the Rolex. But what do we really know about another person's sexuality; and to what extent do we understand its proper place in our lives? My belief, I repeat, is that the post-war world has become almost enslaved to sex, especially in terms of the search for the perfect partner.

It is all too easy to assume that even if advertising and other pressures in our highly-sexed culture did not exist, it would still be *natural* for us to get as much sex as possible. Even behind such statements as 'I'm saving myself' lurks the unspoken thought '. . . for when I'm ready . . . ' In *Sex Is Not Compulsory*, a defence of the individual's right to be celibate, Liz Hodgkinson poses the question, 'Does sexual desire really exist?' Her reply, not surprisingly, is that 'there is no such thing as purely *sexual* desire or *sexual* frustration', and that what 'we call arousal, frustration and mental satisfaction are actually generalised mental feelings that we have in recent times, for some reason, ascribed to the genital area'. Hodgkinson adds that countless people can and do live completely satisfactory and fulfilled lives without ever having physical sex.

> 'Monks and nuns in religious communities are, in the main, perfectly happy and healthy and in fact tend to live longer and succumb to far fewer degenerative diseases, such as cancer and heart conditions, than their peers in the outside world . . . There is no evidence whatever that these avowed celibates live in a perpetual agony of sexual frustration, or that they have to 'relieve' themselves periodically by vigorous masturbation, nor is there any evidence to suggest that homosexuality is more apparent in monastic life than in the outside world. In fact, it appears that celibacy is actually the very easiest of the many disciplines religious people choose to follow.'

Frankly I don't know how to evaluate her ideas. Innumerable people undoubtedly *do* live their lives without sex, and quite contentedly so. But unquestionably, the more you think about sex, the more aroused you become; and within our sexually laden culture, it is difficult to find a spare moment just to contemplate the matter objectively. Shop

71

windows are full of mini-skirted dummies with pouting lips or muscled Rambo-like dummies with gleaming white teeth. The popular tabloid newspapers show an endless succession of breasts, while the subterranean periodicals reveal even more. While people are sticking their tongues down each other's throats daily on television, suggestive advertisements stare down at us from billboards. And now, in the context of 'safe sex' and the sale of condoms, we're lectured about sexual intercourse on TV, radio and in serious news-papers, and almost implored to do it.

Hodgkinson, however, does seem to be partly right, even if inclined to take the matter rather to extremes, for hers is almost an *ideology* of celibacy. Some individuals, I believe, are more sexual in nature than others, not in the sense that they are somehow pro-grammed as such from birth, but that a slight biological difference, mingled with other factors of personality and mind, produces this effect. It seems to me, too, that sexual *desire* must be partly rooted in biology; after all, one of our major functions in life is to reproduce. But this biological desire is tied up with culture. Thus even on a desert island the sight of female flesh *per se* might not necessarily lead to male sexual desire – it could well depend on attractiveness or age. Moreover, arousal as a result of the opposite sex exposing this or that part of the body varies according to culture and period. A man in a Jane Austen novel might well be excited by the glimpse of a well-turned female ankle, whereas the sight of a knee would have been a pornographic impossibility. Nowadays an ankle would hardly excite sexual interest, unless perhaps it were bound in leather thongs.

Where Hodgkinson is surely right, however, is that the move from arousal to sexual action is wholly mental, social and cultural; in other words, subject to individual control. We may feel sexually excited by the appearance of another person, aroused by their conversation, their laugh or whatever, but the impulse to sexual action is a conscious choice. So, if we make an approach, it is because we have *decided* to do so.

Mind games

Lesson number one. The first easy, almost inevitable, guarantee of poor relationships stems from the mind games we play. Not those

72

which John Lennon sang about in 1973. What a peculiar song from our hero – 'Love is the answer and you know that for sure' – fine, but then – 'millions of mind guerillas putting their soul power to the Karmic wheel'! John Lennon, in fact, is a good argument for not being too hard on ourselves. I can sympathise with him, ironically composing 'Imagine no possessions' while sitting in his palatial surroundings, never having to work again. Like him, we are subject continually both to internal and external contradictions. But it is precisely this search for authenticity, for truth, that must be our goal, which is where mind games come in.

Before we ever meet our prospective partners, we have in mind their perfect image, automatically ruling out millions of others from consideration. To some extent this is necessary. As an unlikely parallel, take our perception of colours. According to the psychologist Jerome Bruner, there are estimated to be more than seven million discriminable colours, and in the course of a week we come into contact with a fair proportion of them. But, as Bruner adds, 'Were we to utilise fully our capacity for registering the differences in things and to respond to each event encountered as unique, we would soon be overwhelmed by the complexity of our environment.' And so it is with people. The story of Cinderella is a wish-fulfilment; it rarely happens. We cut out so many options in our lives, partly from necessity, yet not completely.

Most of us meet people of the same occupational level, usually in a confined geographical area, more than likely of the same colour or creed. Within these boundaries we look for that person who conforms to our mental image of the perfect partner. The eventual reality is often disappointment – on both sides. I don't think I'm making too much of this. Just think about it. All too often one hears people say, 'He (she) doesn't really know me', or 'He (she) thinks I'm something I'm not'. Because of the mind games we play – feulled by stereotypes and illusions – people regularly meet people who are wrong for them. But, you might say, this can all be undone by really getting to know one another. Sorry – lesson number two.

Not getting to know each other

I once worked for a man whom I idolised because he was successful, rich, good-looking and, most importantly, had a wife who was absolutely divine. One day he casually told me that he had never, literally, seen her without make-up. It had been a case of love at first sight and today she was more beautiful than when they had first met. Apparently, she would wait until he was asleep to take it off, and always be up before him in the morning to apply another coat. At the time I was extremely touched by her act of devotion.

This is an extreme example of the lengths we are prepared to go to in order to impress. The Kafka of sociology, Erving Goffman, used to point out that we are all in the business of the presentation of self, or the management of our identity. Put simply, we behave in the presence of others as we imagine they would like us to behave, try to be the person we believe others want us to be. And once we've started on such a track it's hard to get off, unless, of course, we're derailed. In the first stages of a new relationship, it's all guesswork. If she's a literary type, he might pretend to be clever and quote Pinter: 'Remember in *The Caretaker*, the marvellous line, "I can't drink Guinness from a thick mug, I only like it out of a thin glass," – it's true, don't you think?' – He will speak more quietly than usual, only leer at her behind her back, and generally present an image of moderation. If, on the other hand, he *guesses* she likes a bit of roughness, he will play the wild man, gulping beer instead of sipping wine, play her a Hendrix tape, swear a lot and pretend to be a modern Jimmy Porter – ruthless, misunderstood but fundamentally right. So which is the real 'he'? Both, of course. The problem arises if *she* wants to continue with *him*. He has to carry on in the way she expects, and she in the manner to which he has become accustomed. This is the real tragedy of 'love at first sight', which does, in a sense, exist. For some it lasts a lifetime, and if they're lucky it could mean a lifetime of contentment. *If they're lucky.* Most of the time, the self we have presented traps us. If we try to be our real selves, they might no longer like us. 'Oh, Shirley wasn't herself last night, she didn't want sex five times'. Perhaps that *is* her, bimbo.

I really do believe that some of us fall in love at first sight, and I am convinced it can be a moment of immense passion and hope. As Roberta Flack put it, 'The first time ever I saw your face, I thought the sun rose in your eyes' – it does happen. The trouble is, of course, once we think that we know the other person and like what we see, it is difficult to change. It's then too late for any truth to surface. In any case, we are impelled *not* to seek any more information or knowledge. When we say 'I really want to get to know you', what we mean is 'Please be like I think and want you to be, please don't change, please don't disappoint me.' So to lesson number three.

The promise

Sounds like a novel by Kafka or a Pinter play, doesn't it? It might as well be for the disturbing lunacy and lack of communication involved. The road to unhappiness and divorce is littered with broken promises. 'But you promised to be faithful, you promised you'd be home yesterday, you promised me things, you promised me every-thing . . . ' Ted Whitehead's play *Alpha Beta*, which first opened at the Royal Court Theatre in 1972, considers the problem of a relationship in which, for complex reasons, one party is immeasurably more committed that the other. The play opens when Frank Elliot is twenty-nine and his wife twenty-six, and then proceeds to show, over a nine-year period, the agonising disintegration of their marriage. After a three-year separation and in the knowledge that his wife has been contemplating suicide, Frank Elliot raises the issue of divorce. They row viciously.

Mr Elliot (*very serious*):	Can I tell you something you won't believe?
(*silence*)	
	I have no wish to hurt you.
(*she looks at him sourly*)	
	I don't want to damage you! I know your quality . . . and I don't want to humiliate you, to cheat you, to exploit you . . . to emotionally destroy you. That's why I left you!
(*silence*)	
Mrs Elliot (*withering*):	Thanks.
Mr Elliot (*dispirited*):	Ahhh.

75

Mrs Elliot (*cynical*): (*Laughs*)	Still the old saviour?
	Listen, the truth is, you do exactly what you want to do and you don't give a bugger who you destroy in the process. So . . . so carry on, do what you want to do, but just don't ask for my blessing.
Mr Elliot:	And what about you? Aren't you trying to force me to do what *you* want me to do?
Mrs Elliot:	Only the things you undertook – vowed – to do!

Having fallen for our perfect partner, we invariably make unrealistic promises. Those who do not break them are somewhat exceptional. I do not want to denigrate the notion, nor do I intend to be overtly cynical. When we promise to love someone forever, we often mean it. Promises can be so powerful, binding us together; and the breaking of promises is much more painful than we like to believe. Recall for a moment your childhood. Remember the anger and frustration, the sadness, the sense of injustice when a promise was broken. And childhood was controlled by promises – 'If you behave, I'll buy you a toy.' Childhood may teach us not to take promises always at face value, but nonetheless we still learn to believe fiercely in them. When we make promises to our loved one, we can reach dizzy heights of love and affection. Such a promise has a number of functions. It may be the final weapon in our interpersonal armoury, used, for example, to convince someone we ought to be loved. It is designed to show how serious we are in our intentions, and also to hold out the prospect of a brave new world unfolding. The aim is not only to predict change – 'One day I'll buy you a house and we'll have children' – but to supply a beautiful and enticing vision of the future. The most important function of the promise, however, is to ensnare, to capture. A promise is a commitment. And because I believe women, by and large, to be psychologically more sensitive and to possess more integrity than men, I am convinced that women treat

Appearances are deceiving.

The New Woman?

Will our children be free from our romantic illusions?

promises more seriously, as contracts rather than fond hopes.

I am still astounded, nevertheless, by the compulsion to make or exact promises when they can only result in unhappiness and disappointment. 'Promise me you'll never go with someone else.' How many times have you heard that? Promises about fidelity and not playing around really imply that both partners must live an inauthentic life. Romantic love, as I have strenuously argued, creates the delusion that *one person* can fulfil our needs. When we promise to be faithful, for example, we promise not to get involved with others who might make us happier, could be better suited to us, and might well need us more than our current partners do. We reject countless opportunities. We turn down more interesting people, more beautiful people, more considerate people, more communicative people. We turn down Sheila, Penny and Kate, Nigel, Mike and Peter – people from Manchester, Leeds, Bristol, New York, Chicago, Paris. For what? To keep promises. Promises based on what we *believe*, or imagine, our partner wants or needs, and vice versa. Too late. Lesson number four.

The Make-up comes off

Before long we're married. Or cohabiting. We are a couple, heterosexual or gay. Everyone wants us to be in a couple. The pressure is tremendous, even within our individualistic culture. Indeed, my cynical belief is that all the vaunted self-awareness, the narcissistic self-confidence and the endless preening, represent not merely a search for authenticity, but also a desire to make oneself a better commodity in the interpersonal market place. Ordinary people are hardly given the choice of being alone. Unless we decide to become a priest, a monk, a nun or a hermit, we are *expected* to couple up. The irony, of course, is that we are always lamenting the loss of our single status – waking up on our own, spreading out in the bed rather than being cramped. And there are occasions, too, when we urgently feel the need for more control over our lives, not simply in practical matters, but sensing that our personality has vanished, merging with that of our partners. Some of us even start to look and sound like our loved ones. When we're not arguing, that is.

I can't help feeling that for most people – if only they'd admit it –

marriage or its equivalent is a great and painful disappointment. In an earlier stage of their marital disintegration, the Elliots, of Ted White-head's *Alpha Beta*, express both disillusionment and resignation.

Mrs Elliot (*ignoring him*):	I've *grown* sick of it. I've grown sick of you, and sick of sex, and sick of love. (*Pause*) I'm sick of all the burning and the fretting, and the weeping . . . I'm sick of the betrayals and sick of the fidelity . . . I'm sick of lies and sick of the truth. I want nothing more of it. I am sick of it all.
(*Long pause*)	
Mr Elliot:	Then why . . . hang on to it?
Mrs Elliot:	Because I've resigned myself to it.

Certainly, the divorce rate suggests I'm right. Assuming most of us choose our partners on the disastrous basis of fantasy, marriage soon becomes boring compared with being single or courting. We are all expected eventually to 'settle down', as my dad never tired of saying to me. What it really means is that 'One day, son, you are going to worry earnestly about money, no longer have any fun, love your children but argue with their mother, and have your freedom restricted.' Please let me reiterate, however, that some, a few, are luckier or more thoughtful than the rest.

Every couple is, of course, unique, but nevertheless there are discernible patterns of behaviour. To begin with, most couples who work and have children are tired. Perhaps this is the reason why, when in public, they spend so much time saying absolutely nothing to each other. Alternatively, they always seem to be squabbling and arguing. And what about leisure? I'd hazard the guess that the men go out drinking more than women, that men do almost all the DIY, and that women do more needlework and knitting. I'd say that as time goes on they both do less public drinking, dancing and listening to music, and that their lives are increasingly dominated by television. Furthermore, married couples invariably abstain from public fun in order to save up for Christmas and holidays in Spain (or France if they are middle class). And that's *exactly* what the statistics show.

What does all this mean? I think we punctuate the relentless boredom of being with someone we don't *really* like by using television as a wish-fulfilment, a belief that life could be like those happy (or sad) people on the screen; or as something simply to take our minds off our unpleasant reality. Men go out more because it is culturally expected that they do so, and because most men still search for potential new partners even if they 'possess' a current but unsatisfactory one. I believe women to be a *little* more realistic than men. They come to learn more quickly that life *without* men *may* be more fulfilling than life with them. Certainly, if society were economically more protective toward women, especially those who are also single parents, fewer would rush lemming-like into relationships similar to those disastrous ones just abandoned.

Christmas and holidays have taken on a cultural importance of staggering proportions. We may well abstain for forty-nine weeks of the year in order to smile at one another and pretend to be happy for a couple of weeks. Christmas not only makes *us* poor and manufacturers rich, it also encourages us to pretend that all is well with us, between ourselves and in the world at large. Holidays serve a similar purpose.

Matters are much worse, of course, for those suffering material and economic deprivation. For such poor souls there is often no escape whatsoever from the grim realities of coupledom. Why am I painting such a negative portrait? Well, marriage or cohabitation, and the expectation of permanent bliss, often coincides with the removal of the make-up. True or truish selves emerge. Deirdre didn't really like boozing at all. Dennis *was* a menace, especially with his broken promises of fidelity. We don't like what we see. But it's too late, and we move to lesson five.

Heartbreak Hotel

Norman Mailer, in his true mysogynist colours, claims that there are four stages to a marriage: 'First there's the affair, then the marriage, then children and finally the fourth stage, without which you cannot know a woman, the divorce.' Well, Mailer could be referring to alimony, and male objections to paying it. Admittedly, it's sexist legislation, but given that men are poor payers after a marriage is destroyed, it has to exist. As a rule it is so inadequate that pressure on the woman to remarry compounds the difficult experience of being alone. In conceptual and legal terms, we are light years away from sorting out the unpleasant muddle of financial responsibility following divorce. And the truth is that everyone suffers from the broken relationship.

In Woody Allen and Marshall Brickman's *Manhattan*, a tale of ordinary hopes and illusions and sadness, Ike (Woody), realising he is hurting Tracy (Meriel Hemingway) in ending their relationship, pleads with her pathetically not to 'stare at me with those big eyes. Jesus, you look like one of those barefoot kids from Bolivia who need foster parents.' Losing someone, ending a relationship, being rejected even by someone you no longer love or never did, *is* a sad event. It is not helped by society which tends to label the occurrence as a failure, shameful or tragic, especially if young children are involved. To some the conclusion of a relationship comes as a great surprise; for many it signals, albeit temporarily, the end of the world, even if it is clearly for the best. Hopes and dreams dashed, having to start all over again, maybe repeating the whole grisly drama. Indeed, the real tragedy for us, our children and ultimately society is our inability to learn from such disasters. Most of us eventually shrug our shoulders, convince ourselves it was just a matter of the wrong man, the wrong woman, that there was too much pressure on the relationship, that we were unlucky, and get out on the streets again. A few kill themselves. But the answer is self-knowledge. Left alone, we can try to know ourselves better, to understand more closely what we need and want, and to find the kind of person who may be able to help. Somehow the pain and suffering we have felt and caused becomes more meaningful. Almost worth it. But as *Manhattan*'s Ike rightly points out to Tracy, we're still in the dark:

'You can't be in love with me. We've been over this. You're a kid. You don't know what love means. *I* don't know what it means. Nobody out there knows what the hell's going on'.

5

'Delicate but not sensitive wallflower, in interesting modern colours, long-stemmed and in full bloom (28), would like to be discovered by connoisseur who would pluck her with gentle hands and care for her forever.'

'And how, especially, do ugly women survive, those whom the world pities? The dogs, as they call us. I'll tell you; they live as I do, outfacing truth, hardening the skin against the perpetual humiliation, until it's as tough and cold as a crocodile's. And we wait for old age to equalise all things. We make good old women.'

Fay Weldon *The Life and Loves of a She-Devil*

Finding a partner, either for a brief or long-term relationship, is usually a matter of luck and perseverance. Some of us are blessed with beauty, intellectual brilliance or magnetic charm, but most of us just struggle along, hiding our bald patches as we go. I believe, however, that at the present time, the search for the so-called 'perfect partner' is even more of a problem, partly because of personal expectations. Let us take the latter first.

I believe the *women's movement*, feminism, or whatever name we like to give to it, in all its forms and ramifications, from childcare campaigners to radical lesbian separatists, has initiated a process which will, one hopes, prove irreversible. Supported by many men, and against a background of cynicism and exploitation, it has struggled against political, economic and social injustice. I believe that in order to create a genuinely democratic society we must first have honest and fair personal relationships. These teach us the values of altruism, strength and truth; and these are the values we should instill into our children.

More and more women, and men too, now look at relationships in a new light. The differences are in attitudes to and levels of sexuality, in the division of domestic roles, in emotional needs and expectations, in the right to have and enjoy things their parents never possessed or wanted. These modern desires stem not merely from the fact that women now have better career opportunities, but rather from the gradual realisation that they deserve equal rights and equal happiness in personal matters. Increasingly, women want men who differ from the old stereotypes. Men have always expected so much emotional support from their women – remember the influence of mother? – and demand so many favours; yet I believe that in traditional relationships most women feel absolute losers. Indeed, Shere Hite's latest mega-survey (1987) reports that the *majority* of women in relationships complain, among other things, that their men do not *communicate* enough with them. These women are not asking for more sex, or even more radical rights, just for their men to talk to them, for genuine companionship.

We have, thank goodness, made some progress since our parents' day. My mother, however tired or stressed, used to struggle to ensure that food was on the table for my father. She toiled to make the house tidy and pleasant for us. She did all the shopping. She mended us when we were broken. She was in the front line when it came to emotional or practical crises, or when difficult decisions had to be made. She was the one who made the world go round, yet it was my father who had to be admired and respected as head of the family. Nowadays, quite rightly, women want more credit for their contributions. Not that everything is rosy. Clearly men and women are little nearer to leading authentic lives. In this age of superficiality, individuals still exchange their personality packages in the name of love. Even so, positive changes, like those I have just mentioned, *are* occurring; and the changing expectations of people, particularly women, represents one of the principal constraints in the formation of meaningful relationships.

There have been slow but decisive changes, too, in the composition of the population. In Britain, among 15-29-year-olds, there is a surplus of 238,000 males relative to females, and it is expected that by the year 1993 this figure will have risen to 284,000. More boys than girls are born each year, but this is no longer counter balanced by a much higher male mortality rate. In previous decades social factors such as world wars and male emigration produced a net surplus of women, and in consequence many women remained spinsters. This situation no longer applies. As Malcolm Wicks of the Family Policy Studies Centre observes: 'In Victorian days almost a third of women never married simply because there were not enough men to go around', but now the 'pattern has gone into reverse and an excess of women is not apparent before early old age'. So what will happen? One likely consequence is that men will stay single rather longer. Indeed, in Britain in 1985, some 37 per cent of marrying men aged 30-54 were bachelors. Another possibility, of course, is that women will develop greater power in relationships as they begin to realise their scarcity value.

The final difficulty in the search for relationships concerns the movement and spread of the population – the rapidly changing map, due to occupational and hence geographical (and occasionally social) mobility. This trend will increase as money and power continue to be centred in particular geographical areas; and such mobility will only cease when we have all been replaced by robots, and live in dark wastelands.

In 1972 Vance Packard, in his *A Nation of Strangers*, drew attention to the gross problems usually created by 'uprooting' and social

83

mobility. His main case study was the USA but he also considered other societies, and his conclusions are certainly relevant to many Western nations. Packard was interested in the forms of uprooting which potentially separate people, and disrupt or disturb their relationships. So, for example, he considers traditional 'occupational uprooting' caused by people moving to new locations; the uprooting that occurs when 'authentic communities' undergo upheavals because of accelerated population growth, or by the processes of urban renewal; and the *sense* of uprooting experienced when people, even if neighbours remain, are moved into high-rise dwellings. Packard felt it a *moral* duty to seek solutions to mobility problems in order to prevent the accelerating fragmentation of families, a trend he considered to be disastrous.

Packard admits the *potentially* positive advantage of frequent mobility. These include the 'broadening effect' on people; the opportunity to make new friends; the chance to escape present frustrations or stagnating situations; the likelihood of economic improvement; the challenge that may well promote personal growth; the possibility of establishing closer family ties and more equalitarian marriages; and, finally, the potentially wider choices in picking a spouse, an occupation or a place to live in. Sadly, however, he does not believe that such things occur and is in fact much more pessimistic. He draws an unfavourable contrast between modern mobility, which is in essence solitary, culminating in the alienating effect of life in a big city, and the mobility of frontier days when those on the wagon trains enjoyed both shared experience and companionship, usually settling in small villages.

According to statistical evidence, over 40 million Americans change their home address at least once a year, and a third of them cross the state or county line in doing so. Furthermore, the statistics suggest that the average American adult moves about fourteen times in a lifetime, whereas in Britain the equivalent number is roughly eight. However, these figures conceal important groups of 'chronic movers' – people who work for large organisations or who have occupations with easily transferable skills. The poor also move, but over relatively short distances. The 'solid working classes' tend not to move much, because of more intensive kinship ties which they are reluctant to break, because they lack the necessary transferable skills and because they tend to be more wary of change and less good at adapting to it.

People who tell us they've moved to London because of their work are invariably 'in computers' (IBM stands for 'I've been moved'). They tend to be on the young side; statistics show the 18–34 age group of any occupation as the frequent movers, and universities and colleges are certainly the breeding grounds for these super-mobile persons. For couples who move together there are invariably problems. Mobility may well increase the emotional dependence of husband and wife (or partners) on each other; yet the loosely rooted lifestyle often places strains on such relationships. But chronic mobility also has a profound effect on the single person. Packard believes that the impermanent pattern of life influences individuals in their approach both to friends and to socialising. Either they resign themselves to relative solitude and segregation or they become instantly gregarious. This culture of 'instant friendship', in Packard's view, is gradually producing a new blandness in human relations. He also believes it encourages a hedonistic lifestyle. Interestingly, and to my mind perceptively, Packard concludes that women find it harder than men to keep relationships bland, and suggests that women are the deeper, more feeling sex.

As a rule we meet our prospective partners at school and university, in the community, at work, through friends, or in leisure outlets. I know people who were childhood sweethearts and who are now married. Whatever turns you on, I suppose, but it does seem rather limiting. I've often met women in pubs and clubs, and have made many an emotional decision while drunk. I don't think I'm unique in this respect. It's much easier to say 'Will you?' or 'Yes I will' in such a condition. Alcohol makes the world seem an easier, more exciting place. More recently, I've come to meet the important women in my life through work, especially as a university lecturer.

Being a lecturer does encourage the Peter Pan complex. I used to attract women who appreciated flippancy and self-deprecation from someone in a position of power. They were disappointed when they found out I was someone rather different.

In my experience public leisure areas are less satisfactory for such encounters; discos are not places of sanity. I imagine that most disco-dwellers are too tired for anything, let alone deep, meaningful exchanges of views or deep, meaningful sexual encounters. But the real problem with such places is that they encourage the promotion of images, of false selves, and of physical packages. You may strike lucky in one or other of these conventional meeting places, but what are the alternatives?

The commercial introduction industry – computer dating, marriage bureaux, personal ads, and such like – has sprung up during this century in the Western world as the answer to those who either seem unable to meet people they like or 'love', or who have consciously decided to be more specific in their choices and to leave less to chance. This is not to say that individuals who join agencies or place advertisements in the press are any more realistic in approaches to their 'love lives' than the rest of us. Indeed, considering that a substantial number of members of such agencies are divorced and widowed, it may be a case simply of romantically replacing a lost partner with another one. But whatever the motive, the selling of the self through personal advertisements is probably the major growth area within the industry as a whole.

Lonely hearts

Apart from the incredible way in which they have burgeoned in the present century, there is nothing particularly modern about personal ads. In 1818 the then Lord Lucan, descendant of the royal branches of Lorraine and Capet and other sovereigns of Europe, advertised himself, stating that he wished to 'contract an alliance with a lady capable from her rank and talents of supporting the dignity and titles which an alliance so honourable would bestow on her'. This custom was well established by that time, but peaked in the late nineteenth century. Today, in Britain and the USA alone, *millions* of individuals each year advertise themselve and/or reply to others. It cannot, of course, be proved, but I believe that the majority are 'genuine' in the sense that they desire a permanent partner rather than endless one-night stands or orgies. Furthermore, I believe that most of the people using the system seek marriage.

The advertisements themselves invariably reflect our existing

86

culture, with all its sexist stereotyping. Harrison and Saeed, having analysed the content of 800 personal ads, concluded, not surprisingly, that women were more likely than men to offer attractiveness, expect financial security, express concern about the motives of potential partners and look for someone slightly older. Men tended to seek attractiveness, offer financial security, profess an interest in marriage and look for someone rather younger. We've all seen them: 'Girl, 26, slim, attractive, faithful, very lively, I'm too feminine, too female, to stay single', or 'Professional man, mid-thirties, own car and house, seeks attractive woman for friendship leading to marriage'. Traditional personal ads all read exactly alike. They provide continuing and relentless evidence that we have, in fact, lost our way. Jean Gonick in her entertaining *Mostly True Confessions:*

> 'The male penchant for the young and slim dominated almost every ad I read, trivialising all the other attributes. Would a man want a schizophrenic neo-nazi if said nazi were young and slim enough? I suspect that he might . . . I'm not stupid; I understand the appeal of the young. Last year I dated a twenty- five-year-old and he was extremely cute. He had a zest for life, tight skin, and was refreshingly unembittered. But the liaison didn't last long and we almost never went out in public.'

There are numerous outlets, each of which reflects the character type of the advertiser, although the majority, as I have suggested, probably seek straight romance. In Britain, for example, they range from *Time Out* and *New Statesman* to *Gay News*. Accordingly the ads vary: 'Girl, seeks lively bloke for dates, gigs, clubs, cinema, nothing serious' or 'Highly articulate, over-qualified, naively trusting Blanche Dubois type, 30s, needs elder and wise friends' or 'Hairy, 35, adman, with own car and house, would like an intelligent, versatile friend 21-25. Prefer non-effeminate non-smoker.' They can be seen either as a positive attempt by the lonely or the discerning to find a person to satisfy their needs or wants, or they can be viewed as a sad, somewhat pathetic endeavour by the lonely to find some happiness in a world which makes it increasingly difficult for them to do so. Or maybe a little of both.

It is true that the system guarantees a measure of anonymity: the advertiser does not have to answer personal questions, as in the case of a marriage bureau or a computer dating questionnaire. It could also be argued, however, that there is no protection either, no positive vetting. Mind you, in matters of the heart there is, in any event, very little protection.

Pink or blue – what are you?

The oldest established commercial agencies or businesses designed to put us in touch with one another are the marriage bureaux. Unfortunately they have never really possessed a good name or reputation: not because of their practices, rather because we are inclined to feel uncomfortable about seeking a marital partner through a third party. It has always been seen as a sign of failure, and the proprietors of such agencies have been condemned either for exploiting human frailty or for providing the means, unwittingly, for the exploitation of the vulnerable by others.

On 7 June 1931 the warnings of the dangers of using matrimonial agencies was proclaimed by *Reynolds News* under the stark headline of 'Don Juan introduced to 93 love-hungry women'. This story referred to the case of Frank Kettleborough of London, a 33-year-old 'charmer and con man', who had been given introductions to 93 women 'hungering for a home', and who had then proceeded to defraud them. Frank had become acquainted with the women through a matrimonial agency and led them to believe that he had done so with the sole view of getting married. By such means, the court report read, he won the confidence of his victims and, in some cases, their love and affection. He would say that he wanted to set up a home for the women he was courting at the time, surreptitiously inducing them to advance various sums of money. Which they did. On the agency's questionnaire he answered most of the standard questions quite briefly and simply. 'What age?' – 'Twenty one to forty'; 'What colour?' – 'Dark or fair'; 'What height?' – 'Five feet to six feet'. But Frank *was* discriminating with regard to one question: 'State what income required' – 'Must have good income'. One of the women he defrauded produced a letter in court from the accused which contained the memorable passage: 'I shall not let you down, for any money you lend me . . . lovie, I could give you a thousand kisses tonight, because I love you.' For his empty promises and multiple cheating Frank was sent down for five years.

The system remains the same. Individuals are interviewed, questions answered, proof of eligibility sought (usually successfully), and boxes of pink and blue cards filed. Pink of course for the girlies and blue for us boys: these people are *not* radical. Then the 'matching' takes place. I've always thought that the marriage bureaux would make an excellent setting for a radio or television sit-com, or indeed a shortish film.

White-lettered credits pop on and off black screen. There is no sound.

A NORMAN A. JOFFE PRODUCTION
Copyright Incisive Films Inc 1987
All rights reserved

MATCHMAKERS

Edited by
Maurice Rosenblum
Produced by
Norman A. Joffe
Written and Directed
by
Bob Mullan

As Marvin Gaye and Tammi Terrell's You Ain't Livin' Till You're Loving' *is heard over the London skyline, images flash on and off: the skyline at dawn, the sun silhouetting Big Ben, the strutting financial buildings, London Bridge, crowded streets, the bobby on the beat, the neon lights of Piccadilly, hotels, lonely people, lonely faces . . .*

Hazel's (voice over): Oh lovely, another absolutely gorgeous day. How many people are we going to make happy today, mmm? It's so hard being a matchmaker (*clearing her throat*),

> but it's such a challenge. It's such
> worthwhile work.

CAMERA ABRUPTLY CUTS TO:

INTERIOR OFFICE IN MAYFAIR–DAYTIME.

Hazel Parkinson, a dark-haired, attractive if somewhat stern-looking, middle-aged woman, is flicking through some pink index cards. The office is sparse save for Annigoni's portrait of Her Majesty.

Hazel (*sighing*):	Doris, what *are* we going to do about Charles? Have you *any* ideas at all?
Doris (*to Hazel, chuckling*):	Well, we could play a practical joke on her and introduce him to Rosemary Blyton.
Hazel:	Be serious. Rosemary was a mistake. We should never have taken her on; I don't know what I must have been thinking about at the time. A 75-year-old divorcee from the Isle of Skye . . .
Doris (*overlapping*):	Who likes Renaissance paintings . . . (*chuckling*) . . . and wants a younger man.
Hazel:	Charles will be here in a minute. I'll just have to spell out some unpalatable truths, I suppose. *Oh God.*

CUT TO:

EXTERIOR, 'HAZEL PARKINSON'S MARRIAGE BUREAU – SUCCESS GUARANTEED' – DAYTIME.

A shifty-looking middle-aged man ambles up some steps to the bureau's front door with its Cupid door knocker. Knocks.

CUT TO:

90

INTERIOR. THE BUREAU–DAYTIME.

Doris (*chuckling*):	He's here . . .
Hazel:	It's *not* funny. Go on, let him in.

CUT TO:

EXTERIOR, THE BUREAU-DAYTIME

Doris:	Charles, how good to see you. Are you well?
Charles (*nodding*):	Can I come in?
Doris:	Please do. Hazel is expecting you.

CUT TO:

INTERIOR, THE BUREAU–DAYTIME.

Hazel is checking her make-up in a small mirror in her handbag. She looks at a photograph of a military-looking gentleman – her deceased husband. She applies a little perfume. She sits bolt-upright in her chair, placing the box full of pink cards centrally on the desk in front of her.

Charles (*offscreen*):	Mrs Parkinson, how good to see you. As always (*chuckling*) . . .
Doris:	Tea?
Charles:	Yes, but no. I mean no sugar, I'm sweet enough (*chuckling*).
Hazel (*clearing her throat*):	Charles. Mr Marlow.
Charles (*interrupting*):	Yes . . . Good news?
Hazel:	Well. It's like this. I have found it extremely difficult, if not impossible, to find a woman who meets your requirements. To find the woman of your dreams.
Charles (*overlapping*):	Why? I'm normal.

Hazel:	Well, yes you are. You *certainly* are.
Charles:	So . . .
Hazel:	Look. The fact is this. There are not many women under 25 years of age who wish to meet a man of your age.
Charles (*overlapping*):	I'm only 60. And I'm as fit as a fiddle. And I'm not poor.
Hazel:	Yes I know, but girls these days want to be independent. Not many of them want, ah well, ah, sugar daddies. I know you are fit – it shows. And I know you have your redundancy money from Saatchi's left; and of course your pension. In any case it's not *just* a question of your age . . .
Charles:	It's not?
Hazel:	No . . . well (*clearing her throat*), it's your interests.
Charles:	My interests?
Doris (*offscreen*):	Sinatra . . .
Hazel:	Excuse me Doris . . .
Charles:	Sinatra?
Hazel:	I'm sorry Charles, but when you insisted that the girl of your dreams had to love Sinatra, and *had*, yes *had* to encourage you in your belief that you are Surbiton's answer to Sinatra, to support you in your new career . . . well it's not on.
Charles:	Well I look like him don't I? And I *can* sing. I just want to make a few bob out of the kissograms. I'd burst through the doors of parties and begin 'I've lived a life that's . . . ' . . .
Doris (*offscreen*):	Yes, we've heard it . . .
Hazel:	Yes, I can see that, Charles. But it's the age-range. Girls under 25 are more into

92

| | Bon Jovi, so my son tells me. So, in a nutshell, Charles, you'll have to change your age requirements. Keep '*must* love Sinatra', just give more women, older women, a chance. Yes? |
| Charles: | I suppose so . . . oh yes, alright. |

CUT TO:

CLOSE-UP OF HAZEL'S HANDS FIDDLING WITH PINK CARDS – DAYTIME.

| Hazels (voice over): | I've got problems, though. I know what . . . |

CUT TO:

BIG CLOSE UP OF HAZEL'S TWINKLING EYES – DAYTIME.

Hazel (*fiddling with ring*):	Ever been interested in stern-looking women; dark-haired authoritative women . . . ?
Charles: (*chuckling*):	Oh yes . . .
Hazel:	Well, we do have such a woman . . .
Doris (*overlapping*):	Rosemary from the Isle of Skye? . . .
Hazel:	Ssh, Doris. No, a new member, very new in fact. She might well do. Shall I tell her 'eight tonight, the American bar at the Waldorf?'
Charles:	Oh yes. How will I recognise her?
Hazel:	You will. You will . . .

CUT TO:

INTERIOR OF BUREAU – DAYISH

Charles leaves waving goodbye to Doris who has escorted him to the door.

93

Jauntily he makes his way to a men's outfitters. Looking puzzled, Doris climbs the stairs.

Doris:	Which 'very new member'? Has she a card? It's not with the blue cards by mistake, is it?
Hazel (*smiling*):	No. Not yet anyway . . .

CUT TO:

CLOSE-UP OF HAZEL APPLYING MORE MAKE-UP.

Gradually we hear Sinatra's voice. Hazel continues to smile. She inspects her teeth. Tightens the slide on her hair. Laughs. Joins in with the song 'I did it my way'. The My Way orchestration swells. The film cuts to the London skyline, but this time it is night, with the buildings and bridges illuminated with thousands of lights. Fades to black background, with white credits popping on and off the screen . . .

Following the credits, and after the logo has vanished from the screen, the continuity announcer merrily confides: 'Well, who is the mystery blind date? Who could it be?'

Britain's (indeed the world's) best-known marriage bureau was established by Heather Jenner in New Bond Street, London, in 1939. Traditionally associated with the privileged, it has, nevertheless, always had working–class subscribers on its books. Indeed, in the early days, about a quarter of the clients were soldiers or working–class people. As Heather Jenner told a *Sunday Express* reporter in 1940, somewhat mysteriously: 'One is a chimney sweep. He signs himself "Yours to a cinder."' Really? 'Yes, at the moment he's walking out with a cock.' Beats me.

Heather Jenner, daughter of the late Brigadier C.A. Lyon, and ex-wife of the (both) deceased Stephen Potter and Lord James (Controller of the Royal Mint), was brought up in Ceylon (Sri Lanka) where her father had been 'commanding the troops'. As Don Ateyo somewhat caustically puts it, the 'grand old lady of premeditated matrimony,

94

Mrs Jenner has been finding husbands for brides since 1939 when she noticed while living in Ceylon the number of tea planters setting off for mother England in search of a wife and returning empty handed'. On returning to England in 1938, she sought legal advice and subsequently drew up the rules for the bureau which are still kept, *in theory at least*, today. Chief among the rules are that clients are interviewed personally and that such interviews are free of charge; that the bureau does not take on anybody unless they are free to marry, which means that if they are getting a divorce they must have the decree absolute; that clients are taken on only if the bureau considers that it has a reasonable number of people to whom introductions can be made; that everyone is charged the same, with the 'completion' fee – as in house purchase – being greater than the registration fee; that the initial fee entitles the client to introductions as and when available, unless the client is not heard from for one year; that no lists or photographs of clients are sent to anybody, and that introductions are given one at a time.

The bureau opened on 17 April 1939, the first client being a retired Indian Army Officer. Mrs Jenner describes one of her first women clients as a 22-year-old ex-deb, the daughter of a 'distinguished professional man' who had been knighted: 'She lived at home, had an allowance from daddy and wanted to meet a man a few years older than she was, possibly in the army (naturally a good regiment) because she would like to live abroad'. Mrs Jenner mused that she could 'imagine her in some pleasant hill station in India wearing a regimental brooch of small diamonds to back up the pearls and talking about all the right things to all the right people'.

Marriage bureaux operate on the basis of two principles: that the proprietors – like Mrs Jenner, and now her daughter – match their clients on the basis of intuition, hence the emphasis placed on the personal interview, and secondly on the basis of *hope*. When the pink and blue cards don't tally, they hope that people will compromise and reduce their expectations. Such proprietors encourage pragmatism.

Over the decades the Jenner competitors have grown in number and, most importantly, there has been the rise since 1966 of *Dateline*, the world's largest computer dating agency. Predictably, Mrs Jenner is disdainful of computer dating – 'Computers ask a lot of damn silly questions – "are you atractive" and so on – trying to make it a science which it isn't.'

Electronic cupid

In February 1965, at Cambridge, Massachusetts, two Harvard University undergraduates launched *Operation Match* which essentially signalled the beginning of computer dating. Questionnaires were distributed among the students of nearby colleges, and recipients were asked a set of rather basic and mundane questions about their personalities, their attitudes and interests, together with their preferences concerning the members of the opposite sex that they hoped to date. The answers were then fed into a (rented) IBM computer – how appropriate – which collated, tabulated and grouped the information, and regurgitated the 'likeliest dating candidates' for each individual. The selections were sent to the participants, together with their telephone numbers, and the rest was up to them. Within six weeks of the start some 8,000 local students had dated their computer choices, and over the next eight months, as word spread through the nation's campuses, more than 90,000 students signed up with *Operation Match*. This bit of fun was assisted in its publicity drive by the ease with which appropriate slogans could be produced – 'condenser couples', 'digit dolls', and 'brides of Frankenstein'.

Other than the development of more lengthy, complex and elaborate questionnaires, the process has remained virtually the same since 1965. And it has been successful, especially in Britain and West Germany, for two basic reasons. Firstly, computer dating has appealed to the general public's unfailing interest and faith in gadgetry and electronics, so much so that some happy couples write to the computers concerned – 'Hi, I'm Amanda. Thanks for sending me Rupert. He's just what I've always wanted.' The argument is that since our health records, bank accounts and credit records are electronically processed, why not our interpersonal needs? And there is the important additional point that the service is anonymous; no one ever has to visit an office to be interviewed. The second reason for its success is the speed with which such modern technology can collect and process data. Consequently the electronic cupid can put more people into its memory and widen users' choices and potential prospects. Now the *actual* task performed by a computer is the simple processing of data. Certain inputs are available, be it a temperature reading or a description of a 'perfect partner'. The machine then processes these items and gives an output such as a signal to control a heater or an address of a 'suitable' individual. This is done by following a precise, pre-planned programme of instructions until the required processing has been performed, the programme itself being produced, of course, by human effort and subsequently subject to human alteration.

In 1980, while waiting at Heathrow Airport, London, for a flight to Mexico City where I was to attend another meaningful conference on the 'theory and practice of landscaping in the new towns', I was flicking through a magazine and saw a *Dateline* ad. I was immediately attracted: 'We know six girls who are waiting to meet *you!*' No, I was attracted intellectually, not emotionally. It seemed a promising subject for my sociology lectures. I must admit I did fantasise that I'd meet hundreds of women through my research, but I never did. I flew off to Mexico thinking of romance, passion, sex and love, only to arrive to scandalous and outrageous poverty. Women sitting on the roadside, their babies wrapped in newspapers with Gucci shops a few yards away selling handbags at astronomical prices. Handbags.

The key to *Dateline's* success has been thoughtful, well-placed, only mildly sexist and costly advertising. With all the goodwill in the world, together with modern technology, it would not have succeeded without the advertising. *Dateline* (along with others) has fought long battles for respectability, principally against the advertising managers of magazines and newspapers. Condemned in the early years to rubbing shoulders in the personal columns of *Private Eye* and *Oz* with pregnancy testers, Chinese masseurs, condom hawkers and karate experts, it has now graduated to costly acceptability ads in national newspapers. The industry is still excluded, however, from television advertising, which amazes me considering that the armed forces can advertise, not to mention alcohol manufacturers – whose products can cause the breakdown of relationships and spread unhappiness, whereas *Dateline* is there to try to *create* relationships.

Dateline's procedure stems, like that of all other computer dating

97

agencies, from its questionnaire, since the information to which the computer responds is derived from it. So the more sophisticated, complex and qualitative the questionnaire, the better, theoretically, is the response. The first ever *Dateline* questionnaire of 1966 was simple yet nonetheless controversial, and reflected the fact that the majority of consumers at that time were students. The controversy surrounded the section which contained questions like: 'Is flogging hardened criminals a justifiable punishment?'; 'Do you agree Communism is a vice and must be eradicated from the face of the earth?'; 'Should we all be free to indulge in premarital sexual intercourse if we so wish?' Since these early days the questionnaires have become longer, more elaborate and, it is claimed, increasingly reliant on the advice of psychologists.

The questionnaire seeks, through a multitude of questions about self, others, activities, etc., to discover whether the user desires a permanent partner – which most do – or one who is rather less permanent. The procedure then attempts to match the former on the basis of 'complementarity', and the latter more on the basis of 'similarity', particularly of interests. There is, in fact, no science here whatsoever. *Dateline* can aim only for *compatibility*; and fair enough. At best, the electronic cupid can weigh up a limited number of psychological and physical prejudices (or desires) and conclude that two people are compatible. Whether that compatibility leads to a successful human relationship is quite another, more unpredictable, question. But it's at least a start. If, say, you want a chunky man of above-average intelligence, under six feet tall, into Bob Dylan *and* Delius, non-smoker, snappy dresser, well-read, who likes children, and is self-deprecating, and *Dateline* produces such a man, good luck. If they don't, give me a call.

So-called *mismatches* occur, of course, quite regularly. Indeed, the act of filling out the questionnaire is in itself an exercise in balancing ego and modesty against expectation. Who is ever going to admit to being unattractive, for example? 'Into Lennon, I said, not Lenin', complained the woman treated to a night of agitprop, tub-thumping and a film about the Tolpuddle martyrs. Or – 'He *was* a non-smoker, he *was* good-looking, but he was a Country and Western freak.'

'I then spent the most boring hour of my life listening to him talk non-stop about his collection of cowboy clothes while he plied me with photographs of other people in western dress . . . I finally made the excuse that I was cold and had to go home. It was in fact true that I *was* cold; we were sitting on a park bench since (a) he didn't drink and in addition I was unwilling to go into a bar with him in case I met anyone I knew and (b) we couldn't go for a drive in my car since he was afraid of travelling by car.'

Female, 40, Darlington

All agencies admit to receiving complaints. They are in the 'people business', so they are inevitably working in a minefield of human expectations, hopes and desires, usually unrealistic. Some agencies, however, are more cynical and exploitative than others, while some proprietors genuinely care for their customers. And in any case, we must not forget that we're talking about businesses, not charities. The prime motivation is the accumulation of profit, not the spreading of mental health.

The main criticism we hear of the introduction industry concerns the matter of *choice*. Surely those who use such agencies are no longer *freely* choosing their partners? Isn't it totally artificial? Are they weird or what? But what is the alternative for people who want relationships and companionship, or desire sex, or are compelled into coupledom? I heard a conversation the other night in a bar, full of young people freely moving round the place. A creep was telling his friends that he only likes women under twenty-five, and that he'd *never ever* date a woman who had children as she would inevitably have stretch marks. Do *you* want to 'freely' meet him?

6

It might well take 'two to tango', but it only takes one to fool around

'I need and want two wives . . . I wish years ago I had found that
I was polygamous . . . I could be passionately married to several
women and be sincere and wholehearted in each case'.

Stanley Spencer

When Anton Chekhov remarked that if we were 'afraid of loneliness,
don't marry', he was pointing to a tragic irony. The marital tryst
which can result in so much fulfilment, hope, happiness and contentment, in fact rarely does. But this is not surprising. From the cradle to
the grave we are told so many 'happy ever after' stories that we come
to believe in them. We expect so much from marriage: that it will fill
our hearts and minds with meaning, that it will provide contentment,
that it will signal the end of our search for happiness. The cohabiting
couple are not so different either. Everyone believes that within the
relationship, espcially within the other partner, lies the solution to all
problems and disquiets. But far from being a 'haven in a heartless
world', marital and family life too often turns into a port of storm.
The statistics of divorce are depressing enough, and extremely familiar. Rather than bore you with statistics, let me offer a very brief
summary of the terrain. Divorce has been increasing steadily since the
end of World War Two, not only in the UK and USA, but elsewhere,
including the state-socialist and communist world. The remarriage

100

rate has continued to rise, although quite recently the interval beween divorce and remarriage has lengthened and the actual rate of remarriage slowed down. However, this is certainly counterbalanced by the increase in cohabitation. Two 1986 statistics, concerning the British experience, are worth noting: firstly that 72 per cent of divorces were brought by wives, and secondly, that there was a 22 per cent increase in the number of third marriages for men.

It *is* misleading, admittedly, to concentrate only on those marriages that formally separate, divorce or dissolve, and that break into little pieces. How many times have we heard people claim that they are 'living a lie'? How many women have we heard say 'if it wasn't for the children . . . '? And how often do we know that our marriages or our relationships are over, how often do we observe unsuccessful relationships in others . . . *yet*, despite this reality and knowledge, we struggle on, we play out the pretence. For many individuals, of course, especially women, there is very little choice in the matter. Our societies *are* organised economically in such a manner that the disgruntled, despairing woman – especially a mother – is not allowed much freedom. And even if there *is* the possibility of economic escape, there are all those other psychological considerations – as, for example, the consequences of breaking the golden rule of coupledom and rejecting the imperatives of romantic love. But it is not that simple either. At the same time as we are engulfed by one ideology, another is stealthily working its way into our brains. This form of mistruth claims that what is really important is *me* – you and I. Us. What really matters is that we have to learn to be ourselves, to understand fully what we need from life, and to go for it, whatever the consequences. But this is nothing but rampant hedonism and irresponsibility masquerading as self-knowledge.

The problem in searching for patterns in marital unhappiness or marital dissolution is that each particular one is unique. What happens when two people come together is quite immeasurable. Even those relationships which appear so bland, so vacuous, so empty, so boring, have within them secrets that are hidden from us. However, we do know – from our own intuition and experience – some of the sources of the problems. Let's start with sex.

Biblical Timothy, who claimed that 'money was the root of all evil', obviously had never dipped in his sexual toe, so to speak. Relationships that involve couples, especially marriage, have to cope with all sorts of sexual problems. They are usually variations on the seemingly simple questions of when, how much and for how long, and with whom? When we don't experience them ourselves, we learn of them from the confidences of friends (or sometimes strangers), we watch them revealed in imaginative or documentary form in films and on TV; and we read about them in the problem pages of women's magazines. As for serious books on the subject, I'm afraid I can't get past the basic terms – indeed I'm convinced that Shere Hite thinks of nothing else than orgasms. But, like everyone else, I'm caught up in the harmful illusions that surround sexuality. The tabloids have fun with such questions as 'How much is enough?' and 'Who's doing it where?', but in fact this is another, if somewhat trivial case, of sexual pressure. From the moment the teenage girl asks 'How far should I go?', it all unfolds. By the time the average relationship has settled down into a sexual pattern, the damage has invariably been done.

We live in a sexist society, no question about it. Men *have* been brought up to exploit women sexually. The double standards are quite pernicious. We 'save' our girls while we 'encourage' our boys. Who, then, are our boys going out with? Scrubbers – somebody else's daughter. Later, the couple are given the three messages of moderation, fidelity and reproduction. Stable, safe relationships will or should consist of moderate sexual activity; each partner should remain faithful to the other; and our goal is to reproduce the species. So what happens? I would honestly claim that in over half of these relationships the result is the very opposite – dissatisfaction, affairs and dissolution.

People have always had affairs, but it seems likely that since the Sixties they have increased both in number and, to an extent, in terms of acceptability. Affairs may gratify the body but they certainly do not help the mind. The hurt is caused not only by the fact that someone is deceived or cheated but also by the secrecy involved. An extraordinary degree of hypocrisy surrounds extra-marital affairs. *Alpha Beta*'s Frank Elliot once again describes it well:

Mr Elliot (*carried away; raging*): Hypocrites! I know how they

102

really look at me when I come down the road. 'Look out,' they whisper. 'Here comes Mr Elliot, the black sheep of Greengate Avenue. Bring in the children and bolt the doors!' And the truth of the matter . . . is that half the men are practising quiet, civilised adultery and the other half are aching for it . . .

The hypocrisy extends beyond the actual practice. There is also mental or psychological adultery. Both partners often wish to be elsewhere, with another person, imaginary or real. It is hardly surprising, therefore, that there are endless communication problems in relationships.

Recent cultural changes, however, have brought somewhat different attitudes to affairs. Some people, *not* a majority, believe that you can stay within a relationship *and* have other meaningful sexual relationships. I do not mean those who lead a life of absolute promiscuity, but those who believe firmly in the duty-to-self ethic. For them the insistence of monogamy in relationships appears hypocritical or old-fashioned, or threatens to reduce it to a condition of stubborn possessiveness. Daniel Yankelovich claims that the old 'double standard made a restricted concession to the male; his transgressions must be limited in number, they must never be flaunted, appearances must be maintained and responsibilities toward the family must not be jeopardised', whereas the new ethos of self-fulfilment 'abhors this outlook as hypocritical and demeaning to women, and is thoroughly rejected'. The trouble, Yankelovich believes, is that this more recent as-long-as-it-doesn't-hurt-anyone norm does not appear to work very well in practice. The disclaimer of 'we both agree we won't hurt each other' turns out not to apply: someone *is* hurt. Most of those self-seekers interviewed by Yankelovich in his research endorsed greater sexual freedom for both partners, but in practice acknowledged that such freedoms strained their marriages or relationships. But this is hardly surprising, given the staggering expectations and obligations placed upon coupledom. Yankelovich argues perceptively that successful relationships, successful marriages, are:

'woven out of many strands of inhibited desire – accessions to the wishes of the other; acceptance of infringements on one's own wishes; disappointments swallowed; confrontations avoided; opportunities for anger bypassed; chances for self-expression muted. To introduce the strong form of the self-fulfilment urge into this process is to take a broomstick to a delicate web. Often all that is left is the sticky stuff that adheres to the broom; the structure of the web is destroyed.'

Put another way, couple relationships may well create a claustro-phobic condition of inauthenticity. Self-fulfilment, either through a change in behaviour, an increase in self-disclosure, or a search for new or different sexual or psychological experiences, may be disastrous. Put yet another way, it is hardly surprising that individuals within relationships feel frustrated.

There is a considerable amount of intuitive as well as academic evidence that men 'fall in love' sooner than women, but that women then 'fall out of love' rather more quickly, though it is fair to add that women also seem more prepared to carry on working at hopeless relationships – 'flogging a dead horse', colloquially speaking, often for sound economic reasons. However, returning to the observation that men 'fall in love' sooner but women 'fall out of love' faster, this of course makes some sense of the double set of statistics that women initiate the majority of divorces, and that there are more men entering third marriages. Sexist as it may sound, men *do* seem to fall for the ideology of romantic love much more than women – perhaps because the unconscious search for the mother-figure is so strong. Further-more, in a patriarchal society, possession of a woman signifies status – hence the frenetic race to get one. But even though women *may* be a little more realistic about men, it is not easy for them to cope with the shock of realising the truth about their 'permanent' partners.

It is often difficult to describe the events that precipitate the breakup of a relationship, and in any case unhappiness in one area tends to spread to the others. Although it may be true that sexual unhappiness is a sure sign that a relationship is doomed, it is usually a combination of various factors. Sexual differences and dissatisfactions: economic disagreements and deprivations; power struggles over children, work and freedom; divergences in personality development – 'growing apart'; communication troubles – men refusing to talk to their partners about personal problems and everyday matters; these are all elements that contribute to the disaster. And the ending of a relationship is indeed disastrous. Even if we *really* know that it is best, especially in the long–term, to end it, when any relationship dies part of us does as well. The oft-repeated 'If he hadn't gone I would have myself, sooner or later', does not lessen the existential, emotional and social pain involved. Even if we do not immediately recognise the fact, self-identity is shattered. Suzanne Gordon, describing the legal ending of a relationship, argues that 'divorce is one of the loneliest of modern rituals', and that 'before, during, and after the actual culmination of the legal process it is an ordeal that rips people away from their roots, their important relationships, and a part of themselves'. She concludes that there is nothing quite like it, 'except perhaps war'.

Coupledom is a cultural product. There are no *natural* reasons that demand we live in any particular way. Perhaps one of the most significant and yet seldom–discussed cultural changes that has taken place and which has increased the pressure on our already fragile relationships, is the simple but profound fact of longevity. Our lives are longer than those of our predecessors, and so, potentially, are our marriages. Formerly, when marriages were shorter, the chances were that death would intervene, forestalling despair. What, then, is the source of our modern tragedy? What makes marriage the 'wastepaper basket of the emotions', as Sidney Webb unkindly called it? It is, as I have beeen arguing strenuously, the ideology of romantic love: the *freedom to choose* the person who will be with you for the rest of your long life.

Where Barry Manilow meets the Houyhnhnms . . .

One alternative to freedom of choice in love relationships is the 'arranged marriage'. In sixteenth–century Europe, for instance, marriage was traditionally regarded as a *duty*, and choice, accordingly, should be on *rational* grounds. And since, within certain well-prescribed classes, parents were more experienced in the ways of the world, it followed that it was they who should choose marriage partners for their children. Similarly, during the amusingly called 'age of reason', it was considered that if marriage between unequals for the purpose of acquiring wealth was a poor foundation for marital happiness, so also were inflamed passions or romantic conceptions of love. Jonathan Swift, for example, favoured matches of 'prudence without passion', and indeed in 1726 extolled the virtues of the Houyhnhnms, the logician-horses of *Gulliver's Travels*. Swift contrasted the behaviour of the Houyhnhnms, who were endowed with reason, to that of the race of man, the Yahoos, who were not. The Houyhnhnms are dignified and conduct their lives with a noble simplicity, while the Yahoos are brutal and disgusting – literally disgusting. Swift's explicit descriptions of the bodily functions and sexual behaviour of these foul and degenerate humans made the critics recoil with distaste. The satire causes poor Gulliver, seeking some evidence of man's nobility, to conclude the very opposite. Swift's purpose in this book was to express his firmly held belief that 'reason' is man's priceless gift.

In contrasting the free choice of mate, as encouraged by the ideology of romantic love, with 'arranged' marriages, we have to be wary: our *choices* are invariably within limits. We are restricted in our choice of potential perfect partners for a number of reasons besides our individual idiosyncracies and prejudices. To begin with, there are the contours and constraints of class and status. It happens occasionally, but as a rule the daughters of multinational merchant bankers do not marry, indeed ever meet, the sons of motor mechanics who are following in their fathers' footsteps. In addition to this process of *elitism* there is the reality of geographic homogamy. As Martine Segalen notes, for example, in the study of marriage patterns in Brittany and Normandy: 'Social milieux still reproduce themselves from within.' In other words, people tend to marry others from within their relatively localised environment. Even with increased mobility, individuals often return home in search of a partner. There are also a number of cultural values which affect our choice, such as the belief that a man ought to choose a woman who is not as tall as he is, and other such crazy notions. Remember the 'new maths?' Another cultural notion is that a man, ideally, should be older, by some seven years or so, than the woman of his life. Why? It may well be that women *are* more mature emotionally and hence can afford to

106

give men a start. But this is a cultural idea, not a psychological truth and for some it imposes a constraint on choice. Furthermore, it virtually guarantees lonely widowhood, given the tendency of males to die at an earlier age. And of course another variation of the 'new maths' tells us sensitive men to dump our middle-aged partners in favour of younger versions.

The historian Alan Macfarlane, in his survey of marriage and love in England, 1300–1840, points out that the idea that marriage is based on personal feeling may strike us as self-evident, but that in the majority of societies marriage is viewed as far too important a matter to be left to the individuals concerned. In peasant societies, for example, marriage is largely based on arrangements by kin, or on the basis of other interests, and the personal feelings of the couple involved are actually of no great concern. As Macfarlane eloquently argues, the combination of 'spiritual love, frustrated sex, and marriage is a uniquely western' phenomenon, and is culturally specific. He asserts that in England from the twelfth to the eighteenth century, and for the bulk of ordinary people, marriage partners were freely chosen, although consultations with their parents *did* take place. The important aspect of the English marriage system – which for centuries set it apart from most others – was the lack of the need for parental consent:

'There was no absolute requirement of parental consent or of a certain age. All persons on reaching the years of puberty were declared capable of wedlock solely on their own authority. No religious ceremony, no record, or witness was essential. The private, even secret, agreement of the betrothed, however expressed, was declared sufficient for a valid contract.'

Therefore a marriage between partners aged seven years or over, without the consent of parent or guardian, and even in opposition to it, was held to be legal. Also extremely important was the fact that marriage, like any other contract, was not valid *without* the consent of partners. So children didn't need the consent of parents but parents needed the consent of children. Naturally there were pressures on the young people of certain families to marry particular individuals. For although the parents did not possess the moral right to influence them, they did nonetheless have the social and economic power to do so.

The tensions that often developed subsequently are recorded in diaries and letters of the period, most of which emanate from wealthy families. In the conflict between 'individual emotion' and 'long-term economic interests', the balance favoured the children of relatively poor parents but not those from rich families. The 'noble' upper classes, not surprisingly, exercised stricter control over love and courtship than did those of the lower classes. In the eighteenth century, however, marriage became less private with the introduction of such conventions as public licences and registers. In Victorian England the upper classes carefully regulated individual choice to ensure both the exclusion of 'undesirable partners' and maximum gain for both sides. As Leonore Davidoff says: 'Social exclusiveness ensured the former' while the latter was 'achieved by the strenuous bargaining which took place after the marriage proposal and acceptance'. Under such a system it was vital that only potentially suitable young people should mix. To meet these ends, 'balls and dances became the particular place for a girl to be introduced to Society'.

When we consider truly arranged marriages, our thoughts invariably turn east, to India. According to the early Hindu scriptures, the marriage system in India was well established in the Vedic period (4000-1000BC) and has been closely adhered to ever since by the vast majority of the population. The traditional pattern did not, of course, allow prospective spouses to participate in the decision-making process of their own marriage. There were no expectations of 'falling in love'. Rather, as Prakasa and Rao put it, 'love was regarded as an uncontrollable and explosive emotion' which made a 'young person blind to reality, reason and logic'. It was argued that family stability could well be threatened if 'love' took over, possibly leading to an unsuitable spouse. The Hindu system regarded individual choice in mate selection as wholly undesirable, fearing that such freedom of choice might make it more difficult for the bride to adjust to her new family. In such extended family structures the arranged marriage is claimed to have the following positive effects: it helps to maintain the pattern of social stratification – the caste system; it secures parental

108

control over other family members; it improves the chances of preserving and continuing the ancestral line; it provides an opportunity to strengthen the links of kinship; and, importantly, it allows for the consolidation and extension of family property.

Such arranged marriages *are* still common but there have been considerable modifications in recent times, especially in the larger urban regions, among the educated youth and among those exposed to the ideology of romantic love – those innocent people, for example, who while listening to the radio in Calcutta or Birmingham happen to hear a Barry Manilow song. Indeed, we hear much of the conflicts, often leading to dramatic breakdowns, between the various generations in Asian families concerning the purposes of love and marriage, and the means of achieving such ends. We hear rather less, however, of the more mundane situations where young people *accept* the principle that decisions affecting individuals should be made by the family as a whole, often despite their personal apprehensions about marriage and resentment of the restrictions imposed upon them by their parents. Undoubtedly, such arrangements sometimes curtail and deny human liberty. Amrit Wilson, in her *Finding a Voice: Asian Women in Britain*, tells awful tales of women suffering pain and violence at the hands of men chosen for them by others. Take, for example, the tale of Surjeet who, despite reservations, went through with an arranged marriage:

'It was arranged through my uncle. He knew somebody or other at his factory. He said, "He is not an educated person but then again you have rejected educated people." I thought, what is education anyway, so long as the person is good and kind, that's what matters . . . (and he was) . . . a completely strange person – I knew I was expected to sleep in the same bed as him. But surely people have got feelings. All I can say is that I was attacked. As soon as I entered the room I was attacked and I screamed. First I tried fending him off but I was so scared. I screamed. I just screamed, called for my mum and dad. The whole house must have heard but nobody came; it seemed that it was going on for hours. Eventually there was a knock on the door. It was one of the wives. I just went to her and clung upon her and I wouldn't let her go. I said, "I can't stay here at all. Please let me sleep in your room." I was really shaking. I was in such a bad state. She tried to calm me, said "Don't be silly" and everything. By this time I had managed to take her out into the living room. Then the oldest brother came and he said, "Either you get back in there or I am going to tell him to come and get you." So I went back in . . . '

It must be noted, however, that most of the women who spoke to Wilson stressed that the arranged marriage was not the tyrannical system so sensationally depicted. In practice, they argued, it is far less traumatic and much more 'semi-arranged'. In other words, the parents might well suggest types of partners or indeed have a particular person in mind, but they would give their son or daughter the right to say 'no'.

Letter to Brezhnev . . .

In pre-revolutionary China one of the most sacred duties of a son was to provide descendants for his and his father's ancestors. Wealthy land-owning peasants traditionally formed marriage ties with other families for political and economic reasons. The poor, on the other hand, saw marriage and children as necessary steps for providing security in old age – the family acted as a kind of welfare service. In post-revolutionary Communist China, however, political policies have aimed to undermine the old family system and the patriarchal ideology supporting it, though not to destroy the family itself as a domestic unit. Marriages are still designed to serve the interests of a larger group, but whereas formerly this group was the family and lineage, it is now the collective or 'society'. Today it is the Party which has the final word on who may marry, and when and how the marriage will be celebrated.

The sinologist Margery Wolf claims nonetheless that in rural China marriage is still viewed primarily as a family event, much as it was in pre-revolutionary days. It is a process which not only transforms children into adults, but also transfers women from one family to another. Choosing a husband is a serious affair, bearing very little resemblance to 'sentimental romance that Westerners associate with courtship'. Rural marriage is a matter concerning families, not lovers. The major changes, of course, have been in the urban areas. In the cities, the State is a more influential force than the family, and, as Wolf explains, 'permission to marry comes from the work unit' Adulthood and marriage are made possible by the State, which provides work, not by the father with his land. Wolf concludes that whereas the 'rural patriarchs have, for the time being at least, kept much of their authority over women and younger generations, among city-dwellers paternal authority has been thoroughly undermined by the State's taking to itself many of the sanctions and indulgences the patriarchy once had exclusive rights to dispense'. Careful choice of a potential partner is therefore essential. Considerations such as morality, character, interests, skills and Party status are just as important as physical appearance.

The purpose of this brief review of marriage traditions in Britain, India and China is to show, quite simply, that the institution of marriage can serve a variety of functions in different societies and thereby determine the styles and techniques of mate selection. Another instructive example of changing attitudes comes from the Soviet Union.

Marx and Engels quite explicitly regarded the marriage system in a capitalist society as being based on the principles of commercial exchange, and condemned the 'market theory' of mate selection. In their view, bourgeois monogamy encouraged the accumulation of capital by ensuring the orderly transfer of property from father to son. And in return for the potential economic worth of their future husbands, women were forced to sell their bodies on a marriage market. Marx and Engels believed that by abolishing private ownership of the means of production, marriage itself would come to be a union reflecting real free choice between partners, without regard to economic considerations. Engels, in his *On the Origin of the Family, Private Property and the State* (1884), foresaw that there would then be 'no other motive left except mutual inclination'. Under communism, Engels argued, love alone, 'by its nature exclusive' and of long duration, would be the basis of marriage. And indeed in the post-revolutionary Soviet Union, arranged marriages were denounced as being exploitative and morally decadent. An instance of this occurred in 1947 when a Moscow theatre presented a comedy about a farmer and his seven daughters, concerning the intrigues in which he became involved as he tried to get the girls married off to eligible military officers stationed in the vicinity. A review of the play in *Trud* was sharply critical:

'In deciding to put on this play, the theatre has rendered a disservice both to the author and to the audience. A great subject has been vulgarised. It would be difficult to think of a more false situation. In our country, people get married according to the dictates of their heart, and not according to the arbitrary will of their parents and superiors.'

The full flowering of such 'free choice', although widely desired, nevertheless has not been easy to achieve. Demographic changes and subsequent imbalances, rapid urbanisation, and the extraordinary rise in the rates of divorce and remarriage are the main factors which have made it difficult for many individuals to marry freely. Indeed, such trends have made it impossible for some people to meet any partners at all. In the country as a whole, there is a gross imbalance between marriageable women and marriageable men. For example, although the male birthrate is higher than the female birthrate, the mortality rate among men aged between 20 and 45 is treble that of the rate among women of the same age. Consequently, by the age of 25-27, the male preponderance stemming from the higher birthrate is eliminated, and beyond this age there is an increasing female preponderance. In some cities there is a very significant surplus of women. Despite this general excess of marriageable women over eligible bachelors, however, there are certain population centres, districts and entire provinces with disproportionately high numbers of men. In many northern cities, for instance, the men quite literally have no one to marry. The same holds true in the vicinity of almost any large construction site (for example, of hydroelectric stations), in some mining towns, and elsewhere. These circumstances undoubtedly help to account for the large percentage of bachelors among mature and older men in the Soviet Union.

In cities with a predominantly *monosexual* population, alcohol consumption, not surprisingly, is far higher; indeed they tend to resemble the 'Wild West' rather than prototypes of what Lenin termed 'Soviet power plus the electrification of the whole country'. The 'cities of bachelors' have to some extent been created by a narrow approach to economic development and the failure to give adequate consideration to social and interpersonal needs.

Frank Clarke's delightful film *Letter to Brezhnev* tried to show that in many respects the Soviet Union is *exactly* like Britain and the USA. Ordinary individuals in the Soviet Union, too, have sexual, emotional and companionship needs, fall in love and, like ourselves, frequently succumb to the ideology of romantic love. Despite certain constraints, of course, individuals try to choose partners on the basis of physical attraction, marry, and then divorce readily and at a massively increasing rate. Indeed, whereas in the USA one in two marriages split up, the parallel figure for the Soviet Union is one in three. And, as in the West, people resort to the introduction industry in an attempt to find a perfect partner. Vladimir Menshov's wonderful 1981 Academy Award-winning film *Moscow Distrusts Tears* contains a scene in which a woman pleads with Moscow Council for support in the running of her marriage bureau. She claims ironically that 'two people met through us, although they lived in the same building . . . it's crazy, this urbanisation.'

7

Where John Wayne meets male tenderness and fighting women

'I don't feel we did wrong taking this great country away from
the Indians. Our so-called stealing of this country from them
was just a matter of survival. There were great numbers of
people who needed new land, and the Indians were selfishly
trying to keep it for themselves.'

John Wayne

Everything I've said so far leads to the inescapable conclusion that
somehow we have *lost our way*, that although we would like to hand
over to our children a world that is healthy and good, with ample
scope for fulfilment and happiness, the reality is somewhat different.
The rising divorce rate, the frequent feeling of emptiness and the
relentless struggles of the gender war are merely three symptoms of a
deeper social malaise in which meaning and purpose seem to be
absent. But surely, you might say, there is room for optimism. Are
we not in the early stages of creating 'new' men and women – people
who both feel and behave in ways that run counter to tradition? But is
that true? And how do we propose finding out – a national or
international survey comparing modern behaviour with that of our
parents? Or should we simply take a look around us, at our communities, our families, our friends? My assumption is that the 'new man' is
no more than a journalistic term designed to produce copy and fill

114

space, rather than a symbol of genuine personal and social change. I see people around me behaving more or less as they have for the past 35 years. But the concept is much more plausible for Mark Gerzon, an American historian who envisages the wide-scale emergence of 'new men'.

In his account of the 'changing faces of American manhood', published in 1982 as *A Choice of Heroes*, Gerzon states that to be a male hero, a man should either avoid becoming entangled with women altogether or should marry a woman who remains obediently in the background. It is, he adds, 'as if man becomes heroic by virtue of the distance he places between himself and the feminine'. This is, of course, true, and writers like Robert Johnson, as we saw earlier, believe that this distance must be reduced in order to mould new *people*, let alone new men. Gerzon's own hope is that we will respect diversity: 'To replace an old stereotype with a new one would be pointless . . . the range of masculinities and femininities is wide, so wide that the qualities overlap. Who would wish that all men were passive any more than one would wish that they were all aggressive?' His new men, therefore, would differ not only from past archetypes, but also among themselves. You will 'know them when you meet them', and they will not 'make you feel besieged, but befriended; not depleted, enriched; not used, understood; not dominated, served'. By this definition, my friend Alex is a 'new man'. He cares about others before himself, but is not so altruistic as to submerge his own needs and personality in that of another person. And like the men in a number of Bruce Springsteen's songs, he exudes male tenderness; he considers weakness and vulnerability to be positive virtues, yet by recognising this fact, he feels he will become strong. Alex talks about himself, his hopes and dreams, his fears and worries, his abilities and shortcomings; he talks with women, not at them. He is extremely emotional, open and honest, and regularly hurt; he is still, nonetheless, a man. On the other hand, I know men who can only be *exploitative* in relationships, who believe that women need men more than vice versa, that men *give* sex to women, that women belong in the home, and other such platitudes. But this is hardly surprising in a culture which advertises toys of war and violence for our little boys, while selling dolls that wet themselves and cry to our little girls.

The pernicious influence of advertising and of the mass media on the minds and behaviour of our children cannot be underestimated. To take one example: in the USA, children aged between 2 and 11 years old are exposed, on average, to more than 20,000 TV commercials annually (including those directed at adults) of which 7,000 are for sugared cereals alone! The situation is so crazy that the major broadcasting networks have increased the number of their paid public-service announcements in order to give children more balanced nutritional information. And when our children are not receiving messages designed to make them toothless, the boys are provided with examples of male strength and violence, in addition to robotic intelligence, while the girls are invited to look on Barbie as the ideal in feminine beauty.

Once these seeds are sown in their brains, they are subjected to exploitative advertisements depicting men as heroes and women as passive sexual objects and domestic serfs. Not that most children have to venture outside the home anyway for such messages. A recently published survey finds, not surprisingly, that despite 'important social changes, particularly greater female employment, it is still women in families who undertake the great bulk of housework, cooking, child care and – increasingly – the looking after of elderly relatives', and that 'today many combine these tasks with outside work'. It adds, however, that men work longer hours in employment and still contribute most of the family income. The survey concludes that despite 'occasional sightings', the much-hyped new man remains a 'rare species'.

Although the survey in question is devoted to a study of British habits, it is, I am certain, applicable on a more global scale, certainly across the Atlantic. Until the advertising industry is completely controlled, it will continue to reinforce our existing prejudices about the 'proper place' for men and women, and the kinds of lives they should lead.

While Tammy Wynette sings Stand By Your Man . . .

Traditional Country and Western music interests me, not because of the six-shooters, the boots and the hats, but because it so often accurately describes the situations that most women end up in and the problems they face. The solutions it offers may be unpalatable, with the woman deferring once more to her man, but it *is* in touch with the life of ordinary people. *Stand By Your Man* is a good case in point – an anthem to traditional gender roles. It makes men feel big and strong, and women cosy and protected. Of course, you and I are different. We listen to Joan Armatrading, Chrissie Hynde or in the extreme even Dory Previn, should we be feeling particularly masochistic and in need of womanly support. We dance to Madonna, hoping not to hear the lyrics. The point is that women as well as men are prey to messages that encourage them to stay in their traditional-sex-object-domestic- slave-role. In other words, it is very difficult to create 'new men' when we are still surrounded by 'old women'.

In a patriarchal society, one which refuses to value and respect human sensitivities, the men do call the shots but many, many women gladly comply. I know women who abuse gays and lesbians, who are politically reactionary, who allow themselves to be sexually exploited, who treat men as sexual or economic objects. They should know better, but they choose not to. With more 'new men' we will produce less 'old women', and as we reduce the stock of 'old women' we will create more 'new men'. When George and Ira Gershwin put their deliberately ironic *The Man I Love* into orbit in 1956, they spoke of traditional hopes which resulted in both men and women being trapped and ensnared: 'Some day he'll come along, the man I love, and he'll be big and strong, the man I love, then when he comes my way I'll do my best to make him stay . . . He'll build a little home that's meant for two, from which I'll never roam . . . ' Starting from the adolescent moon-June cliché, it admits that the dream, though echoing the cravings of the human heart, isn't likely to come true. The song tells us that although the girl won't find her Prince Charming, she'll almost certainly find a man she mistakes for one; and that the mistake matters less than the fallible aspiration. I shall never tire of hearing Billie Holiday singing those memorable lines; but considering the potency of such notions as they float in and out of our minds, we surely need to promote a different kind of cultural message.

Barbara Ehrenreich, Elizabeth Hess and Gloria Jacobs believe that dramatic changes have already occurred. In their stimulating *Re-Making Love: The Feminization of Sex*, they argue that a *women's* sexual revolution has been taking place, and that its consequences are only now emerging:

'For most Americans, the "sexual revolution" is what Gay Talese found when he set out on his quest to see what middle-aged, middle-class men had been missing all these years; wife-swapping clubs, massage parlors, Hugh Hefner's harem of bunnies, *Screw*. It was a sexual marketplace that dominated and marginalized women; and if this was all there was to the sexual revolution, then its critics have been right to see it as little more than a male fling and a setback for women . . . But the sexual revolution that Talese found is only half the story, or less. There has been another, hidden sexual revolution that the male commentators and even the feminist critics have for the most part failed to acknowledge: this is a *women's* sexual revolution, and the changes it has brought about in our lives and expectations go far deeper than anything in the superficial spectacle of sexuality we have come to identify as "the" sexual revolution.'

Their argument is that men actually changed their sexual behaviour very little in the decades from the Fifties to the Eighties. They 'fooled around', got married, and often fooled around some more – 'much as their fathers and perhaps their grandfathers had before them'. Women, on the other hand, were altering their sexual behaviour so drastically that, for example, the symbolic importance of female chastity is now rapidly disappearing. They not only came to have more sex and with a greater variety of partners, but also had it on their own terms, enjoying it as enthusiastically as men. Indeed, the authors – in the vein of 'Hiteism' – quote a 1975 survey revealing that 81 per cent of their 100,000 female respondents were orgasmic 'all or most of the time'.

Ehrenreich, Hess and Jacobs claim that this *real* sexual revolution has accomplished a number of things: it has challenged the old definition of sex as a merely physical act, specifically a 'two-act drama of foreplay and intercourse which culminated in male orgasm and at least a display of female appreciation'. This traditionally phallocentric version of sex is, in the authors' view, an imitation of rape. Another achievement is to have established a woman's *right* to pleasure. By taking a more active role in sex, by allowing themselves pleasure, they could begin teaching men to abandon their phallocentric attitudes. The authors conclude perceptively, if somewhat brutishly, that heterosexual sex, and especially intercourse, is a 'condensed drama of male domination and female submission'. Or as they graphically put it: 'The man "mounts" and penetrates; the woman spreads her legs and "submits"; and these postures seem to ratify, again and again, the ancient authority of men over women.' They are, sociologically speaking, correct; and their account is extemely thought-provoking. But I cannot believe totally in their interpretation. It is too simple to talk of pure male domination and exploitation. *Symbolically* it may appear to be just that: power and submission. But *in reality* the act is far less purposeful; there is more uncertainty, more vulnerability involved. I cannot believe that women consciously 'submit', nor that on most occasions men deliberately penetrate in order to exercise power with a view to exploitation. Indeed, many men are fearful of sex, and somewhat wary of its promised expectations. And the 'new sexually liberated woman' is about as difficult to pin down as the 'new man'. It is safe to say, however, that along with the oral contraceptive pill, the women's movement has raised the expectations, including the sexual expectations, of many women. And perhaps this attempt to bring about sexual democracy *is* the 'new sexual revolution'.

It is abundantly clear that democracy and the equalisation of rights do start in bed. The personal *is* the political. But I should not want the new sexuality to become a burden, or another commodity to buy and sell. And I would also like to begin chipping away at some other prejudices. Take the case of 'one night stands'. We're told that they are unfulfilling and morally undesirable, except, of course if you carry on seeing the girl: if you don't it was *bad*, if you carry on seeing her it was *good*. If it leads to marriage, it was a very good start.

So tell me who I see, when I look in your eyes; is that you baby, or just a brilliant disguise . . . ?

I think Bruce Springsteen is being rhetorical in his magnificent

Brilliant Disguise as it's clear that he knows the answer. Bruce's realisation that beauty is only skin deep, that personalities and 'character' have to be searched for, is not shared by everyone, especially men. So what we need to learn from women is not solely a new sexual charter, but rather a willingness to go further and deeper into relationships, indeed an extension of what is sometimes called their *relational potential*. The American feminist Nancy Chodorow argues controversially that this 'relational potential' stems from the fact that mothers treat their girl-children as a continuation of themselves, while they regard their boy-children as separate from and *other* than themselves. Because of this differential treatment, the primary attachment for most women throughout life remains the mother. As a result of this prolonged maternal attachment, girls/women develop a particular capacity to form and sustain relationships – the relational potential. Girls/women are better able to empathise with others because they have not had early experiences of sharp separation. The sense of unity is carried through to maturity and adult life. This seems to me a plausible explanation for the commonly observed fact that women tend to make better friends than men.

Not all women, of course, realise their potential. Indeed, it is saddening to see women sometimes rejecting their own gender in favour of men; but this particular pattern of male priority is largely caused by social pressure – 'Catch a man as soon as you can, it's the most important thing in your life.' Perhaps the priority given to opposite-sex *liaison* over same-sex *friendship* is a reality of our present culture, but it certainly need not be. I believe that the female capacity for friendship tells us a lot about the differences between men and women. In a nutshell, I am convinced that in relationships women want to be friends first, lovers second, whereas with men it tends to be the other way round. As Chekhov puts it in *Uncle Vanya*: 'A woman can become a man's friend only in the following stages – first an acquaintance, next a mistress, and only then a friend.' Men want things to happen too quickly, tend to rush in, are more easily fooled; women tend to be better judges of personality and appearance – are able to penetrate the masks we wear. If men had greater relational potential we would spend more time in friendship and less in pseudo-love affairs, or the vain quest for possession of a personality package.

120

I have not so far mentioned gay lifestyles in this book. Quite simply, this is because I feel that there is no great need to differentiate gays and non-gays in this context. Both sets of people may or may not fall prey to romantic love, may or may not be promiscuous and so on. Our general lack of knowledge about gay lifestyles is extraordinary and alarming; alarming because of the way misconception and mistrust can lead to prejudice and cruelty. Like heterosexuals, most gay men and women desire perfect partners, in order to achieve emotional fulfilment and contentment. Some take longer than others to settle down, trying out more potential partners, and many fail in their relationships and suffer pain. There *is* one vital difference, however, as Jean Gonick suggests:

'I thought of Barbara, a dear friend forty years of age. She switched sexual allegiances at thirty, after a ten year marriage. "The best thing about being gay," she had told me, "is that when I'm angry with Sharon, I'm angry with her on a personal basis only. With my husband, it was personal *and* political anger. Sharon and I don't have to fight the gender war."'

I could live, I could die, I could be reborn in your arms . . .

Sings Boy George, androgynous man. Nearly all of us seem to desire intense emotional and sexual relationships, culminating in the discovery of a perfect partner. This search has become more difficult as a result of the shifting contours of the population, the increase in social and geographical mobility, and our own changing expectations; and our epoch has also thrown up additional constraints, dilemmas and challenges.

Since the arrival on the scene, around 1960, of the oral contraceptive pill, our lives have never been quite the same. The pill remains, at least in the industrialised West, the most 'popular' method of contraception among women, although its use fluctuates with publicity about the attendant health risks. Sadly, it is estimated that about half the women who employ oral contraception are using it wrongly and at some point risking pregnancy. The pill, we were told, gave us sexual freedom. True, it gave women more freedom to explore their sexuality, but it also gave men yet another excuse to avoid their emotional and sexual responsibilities.

This same period has seen the virtual disappearance of syphilis but at the same time the terrifying rise of herpes as a major health problem. And, of course, AIDS. In the wake of the hysteria created by AIDS, we seem to have forgotten all about herpes unless, of course, you happen to have it. Herpes and AIDS have altered the contours of sexual behaviour for many people. Fear of AIDS is clearly changing sexual attitudes and practices. I have a friend who is terrified of death; therefore she is afraid of AIDS: therefore she no longer has any kind of sex, with anybody. This may be an extreme reaction. I personally don't care about life enough to worry unduly. But our behaviour *will* change, especially when the manufacturers of condoms realise the profits that can be made, especially with the subsidised advertising they will receive through governments. I suspect that once it becomes abundantly clear that AIDS is as much a heterosexual ailment as one that affects gay people, there will be an accelerated alteration in sexual behaviour. Individuals will cling on to their virginity a little longer, will have fewer partners, and will utilise condoms more; in other words, practise 'safe sex'. Others, of course, will do nothing of the sort. Some men and women could not care less about possible risks. In any event, sexual desire and sexual behaviour are not always under our intellectual control: there are times when irrationality takes over, we act illogically, we are driven solely by passion. Indeed life would be poor if we did not occasionally let passion take hold of us.

The critical question, it seems to me, is whether or not the spectre of AIDS motivates us to reflect upon the role of sexuality in our lives; whether AIDS causes us to think about celibacy, abstinence and the balance or imbalance of the sexual and non-sexual aspects of our lives. Will the reality of AIDS make us consider our own priorities? The threat of increasing disablement and death could help us to get sex into proportion mentally and psychologically as well as practically. It could be a means of getting rid of the pernicious sexist advertising that surrounds us, of bringing realism and discernment to our quest for perfect partners. I doubt, however, that AIDS will have this effect.

122

We will continue to scapegoat gays or find new scapegoats, we will continue to believe 'it won't happen to us', *we will not alter the agenda*. We will refuse to admit that it is *sex itself*, in the manner and extent that it is currently packaged, which is the problem and not the diseased partners we may come into contact with. We humans are capable of great delusions.

I am not, I might add, advocating celibacy, nor am I simply extolling monogamy; I am merely suggesting a reasoned moderation and balance in our sex-laden and exploitative culture. Like Mailer's Bob Hearn of *The Naked and the Dead*, I continue to be sensual and optimistic:

> 'Still there are moments. Different women, different nights, when he lies in embrace, steeped in a woman's flesh until the joy is intolerably joyous. There are love harvestings, sometimes months in a row when there is one woman, one affair, and a proud secret knowledge of each other's loins, admirable matings, sensitive and various, lewd or fierce or dallying gently, sometimes sweet and innocent like young lovers.'

Was Bertrand Russell right?

As the existentialist philosophers never tire of telling us, we humans are *condemned* to live, so we must ceaselessly create reasons for living. We have to *create* meaning for ourselves in order to explain or understand our lives, the lives of others and the world we share. There are no given rules for living, for the realisation of happiness. It is up to us to make rules and find happiness. In terms solely of our emotional, sexual and companionship needs, I believe our age suffers from three great illusions: that we have one predestined lover and partner whose love will make us happy and who will never leave us; that sex, especially sexual freedom or sexual promiscuity, is essential to our fulfilment as mature adults; that *we* individually, are the most important people in the world. All these illusions stand in the way of our finding 'real love'. I believe in 'real love', but would not go along with writers like Johnson and Peck in defining it as spiritual love. Nor, moving though they are, can I agree with Bertrand Russell's thoughts on the subject:

> 'The centre of me is always and eternally a terrible pain – a
> curious wild pain – a searching for something beyond what the
> world contains, something transfigured and infinite – the beatific
> vision – God – I do not find it, I do not think it is to be found –
> but the love of it is my life – it's like passionate love for a ghost.
> At times it fills me with rage, at times with wild despair, it is the
> source of gentleness and cruelty and work, it fills every passion
> that I have – it is the actual spring of life within me. I can't
> explain it or make it seem anything but foolishness – but
> whether foolish or not, it is the source of whatever is any good in
> me.'

I believe that human companionships based on physical attraction *as well as* psychological understanding and appreciation, on empathy and altruism *as well as* sexual pleasure, are the hub of life. But I also feel that we must totally respect individuals who choose a solitary or celibate existence. Those people who constantly seek self-fulfilment are also entitled to their own lifestyles but in so doing will probably create even more problems for themselves. Their definition of the 'good relationship' is even narrower than that of their parents. The ethic of commitment is usually too strong for most of us to adhere to – and in any case a totally committed relationship implies dissociation from the community at large. I would like to see a world with more sexual honesty; not necessarily in the sense of complete openness, which could eventually prove oppressive, but acknowledging, say, that it might be possible to enjoy more than one sexual relationship whilst sustaining one permanent emotional relationship. The burden of fidelity is too heavy a price for most of us to pay. There is no need for a stark choice between the ascetic and the dionysian. Sometimes we have to retire from the world, at other times we have to plunge headlong into it. Similarly, we should not strive to be logical *or* emotional; they are one and the same thing, and it is the sign of the wise man to recognise this. As Gotthold Lessing aptly observed: 'A man who does not lose his reason over certain things has none to lose.'

124

Love is a many splendoured thing . . .

'Many splendoured' because of its great equalising effect. Love does not discriminate between class and race, between rich or poor. There can be wealth with no love; and there can be love where there is poverty. *Real love cannot be bought.* But, unlike the Robert Johnsons of this world, I don't want to make it out to be more than it is. It is a psychological, emotional, social and moral condition we have invented to make life bearable. Some of us are better at acquiring it than others. Some of us simply cannot escape illusions. But I do believe we all really want similar, quite simple things. As Jean Gonick again reports: '"You know why you're really lucky?" she asked. It was Robert's turn to shake his head. "You get to make love to someone you actually know and like and who won't give you a fatal disease".' Provided, of course, we do not turn an *opportunity* – for that is what love is – into an exclusive and possessive affair which can only lead to a less than full life.

We must create better personal relationships so that we can produce better people who can in their turn change the world. But we shouldn't be too hard on ourselves. Love, like life, is hard. We should enter relationships with that in mind. As Jimmy Porter, John Osborne's obnoxious, pathetic yet heroic character of *Look Back in Anger* puts it:

> Jimmy: (*in a low, resigned voice*) . . . It's no good trying to fool yourself about love. You can't fall into it like a soft job, without dirtying up your hands . . . It takes muscle and guts. And if you can't bear the thought of messing up your nice, clean soul, you'd better give up the whole idea of life, and become a saint. Because you'll never make it as a human being . . .

There is much luck involved in love, and many unpredictabilities and mysteries lurking around. Mysteries that even eminent scientists such as Doctors Goldberg and Anderson cannot fathom.

On the shores of Lake Michigan, Drs Goldberg and Anderson relax, snorting cocaine and reading an obscure academic journal.

Dr Anderson	What's the next project, Michael?
Dr Goldberg	Life. *Life*, Larry.
Anderson (*puzzled*)	*Life*. But that's a biggy, Michael . . .
Goldberg	It is, but we can handle it.
Anderson	Any ideas . . . experiments . . . hypotheses . . . ?
Goldberg	Fuck all.
Anderson (*aghast*)	Fuck all? But . . .
Goldberg (*interrupting*)	You see you're still in the Fifties. You still believe there *are* things to *know*. There's nothing to know.
Anderson	So why are we doing *life*?
Goldberg	Money.
Anderson (*sternly*)	But look, Michael, there's a lot of mystery we've got to explain . . .
Goldberg (*overlapping*)	Exactly. It's such a mystery, *anything* you say sounds new.
Anderson (*sighs*)	Brilliant. I do love you.
Goldberg	I love you *too*.

After another quick snort the Doctors pack their car and drive into the lake, under the water and disappear from view . . .

END

Notes

For full details of titles and publishers of authors' works quoted below, please refer to the bibliography.

p. 2 Norman Mailer in the *New Yorker*, October 23, 1948.

p. 4 Philip Larkin (1983),p.48.

p. 5 For a discussion of the purposes of Mailer's work see, for example, Jennifer Bailey's (1979) *Norman Mailer : Quick Change Artist*, Macmillan: London.

p. 9 'Worry',p.21 in Roger McGough's collection (1987) *Melting Into The Foreground*, Penguin: Harmondsworth.

p.10 Edward O. Wilson (1978),p.xiv.

p.11 David Barash (1978),p.295.

p.11 ibid.,p.290.

p.12 Robert Hinde (1982),p.250.

p.12 May Sarton (1985),p.23.

p.13 Glenn Wilson and David Nias (1977),p.12.

p.14 Ted Polhemus (1978),pp.22-23.

pp.18-19 Steve Duck (1983),p.9.

p.19 ibid.,p.11.

pp.20-21 ibid.,pp.39-40.

p.21 ibid.,p.67

p.21 ibid.,p.118.

p.23 Ray Gosling (1980),p.179.

p.25 For criticisms of the 'sixties' see, for example, Peter Berger, Brigitte Berger and Hansfried Kellner (1977),p.195.

p.26 Frank and Fritzie Manuel (1979),p.808.

p.26 Theodore Roszak (1970),p.4.

p.26 Richard Neville (1971), p.206.

p.26 ibid., p.114.

p.26 Andy Warhol and Pat Hackett (1981), p.294.

p.27 Charles A. Reich (1972), pp.13-16.

p.28 Joan Didion (1979), p.87.

p.28 Tom Wolfe (1976).

p.28 Christopher Lasch (1978).

p.28 Richard Sennett (1977).

p.29 Edwin Schur (1976).

pp.29-30 Martin Gross (1978), p.6.

p.30 See Bob Mullan (1983) *Life As Laughter: Following Bhagwan Shree Rajneesh*, Routledge and Kegan Paul; London.

p.31 Christopher Lasch (1978), p.4.

p.32 ibid., p.15.

p.32 See the account of *The Big Chill* offered by Kim Newman in *Monthly Film Bulletin*, Volume 51, 1984.

p.33 Christopher Lasch (1978), p.27.

pp.33-34 Richard Sennett (1977), p.259.

p.35 Daniel Yankelovich (1981), p.250.

p.35 Marshall Colman (1982), p.38.

p.35 Arlie Russell Hochschild (1983), pp.195-196.

p.36 Francesca Cancian (1987), p.3.

pp.37-38 ibid., p.5.

p.39 Joni Seager and Ann Olson (1986), p.3.

p.41 Philip Larkin (1983), p.54.

p.42 Milan Kundera (1984), p.7

pp.44-45 Zick Rubin (1970), pp.265-273.

p.45 Fromm (1975), p.9, *passim*.

p.47 M. Scott Peck (1987, orig. 1978), p.81.

p.47 ibid., pp.90-91.

p.48 ibid., pp.91-92 and pp.97-98.

p.48 Robert Johnson (1983), p.ix.

p.49 ibid., p.18.

p.50 ibid., p.xii and p.61.

pp.50-52 ibid., p.133.

p.54 James Lynch (1977), p.181.

pp.54-55 ibid., pp.60-61.

p.56 Irving Bieber (1964), footnote in *Time*, p.213.

pp.56–57 Ronald Maris (1981), p.112.

p.57 ibid., p.298.

p.58 Suzanne Gordon (1976), p.15.

p.58 ibid., p.38.

p.58 Robert Weiss (1973), p.4.

p.59 ibid., p.4.

p.59 Jenny de Jong-Sierveld and Jos Raad Schelders (1982), p.106.

p.60 G. Zilboorg (1938).

p.60 Harry Stack Sullivan (1953).

p.60 Frieda Fromm-Reichmann (1959), p.3.

p.60 Robert Weiss (1982), p.77.

p.60 Carl Rogers (1973).

p.61 William Sadler and Thomas Johnson (1980), p.38.

p.62 Joseph Hartog (1980), p.2.

p.61–62 Paul Tillich (1980), p.548.

p.62 Clark Moustakas (1961), p.24, p.ix and p.59.

p.63 Claude Fischer and Susan Phillips (1982), p.36.

p.63 Clark Moustakas (1961), p.70.

p.64 Suzanne Gordon (1976), p.33.

p.64–65 May Sarton (1985), p.6, p.64, p.89 and p.168.

p.67 Christopher Lasch (1978), pp.72–73.

p.68 The sub-heading 'pornography is the theory and rape is the practice' is the central thesis of Robin Morgan's (1980) book. As she quite correctly points out the *violence* is already in the pornography in its representations.

p.68 As reported to *Spare Rib* and in Root (1984), p.56.

p.68 John Downing (1980), p.132.

p.68 Jane Root (1984), p.55.

p.69 Janice Winship (1980), p.218.

p.69 Estée Lauder, quoted in Downing (1980), p.135.

pp.69–70 Betty Friedan (1965).

p.70 Wayne Alexander and Ben Judd (1978), p.50.

p.71 Liz Hodgkinson (1986), p.15.

p.73 Jerome Bruner, Jacqueline Goodnow and George Austin (1956), p.1.

pp.75–76 Ted Whitehead (1972), p.67.

p.78 ibid.,p.43.

p.79 On the statistics of married life see *Social Trends*, HMSO: London, (1986), Volume 16, pp.160-168.

p.82 Fay Weldon (1984), *The Life and Loves of a She-Devil*, p.10, published by Coronet.

p.84 *Family Policy Studies Centre* bulletin, 1987.

pp.84-86 Vance Packard (1972),p.180,*passim*.

p.87 A. Harrison and L. Saeed (1977),p.257.

p.87 Jean Gonick (1987),p.37.

p.95 Don Ateyo (1973),p.12.

pp.95-96 Heather Jenner (1979),p.8. See also Bob Mullan (1984).

p.99 For criticisms of and complaints about *Dateline* see Bob Mullan ibid.

p.101 The two 1986 marital statistics are taken from the introduction to John Haskey's 'Trends in marriage and divorce in England and Wales: 1837-1937', *OPCS*, HMSO: London.

pp.102-104 Ted Whitehead (1972),pp.53-54.

pp.103-104 Daniel Yankelovich (1981),p.77 and p.76.

p.105 Suzanne Gordon (1976),p.136.

p.106 Martine Segalen (1986),p.143.

p.107 Alan Macfarlane (1986),p.7 and p.125.

p.108 Leonore Davidoff (1973),p.49.

pp.108-111 V. Prakasa and V. Nandini Rao (1979),p.12.

pp.109-110 Amrit Wilson (1978),p.104.

pp.110-111 Margery Wolf (1985),p.229.

pp.111-113 For a discussion of marital choice in the Soviet Union see, for example, Wesley Fisher (1980) and Vladimir Schlapentokh (1984).

p.115 Mark Gerzon (1982),p.125 and p.262.

p.115 The survey concerning the 'new man' is taken from *Inside The Family* (1987), Family Policy Studies Centre: London, p.66.

pp.117-119 Barbara Ehrenreich, Elizabeth Hess and Gloria Jacobs (1987),pp.1-2,p.193 and p.203.

p.120 Nancy Chodorow (1978).

p.121 Jean Gonick (1987),p.139.

p.123 Norman Mailer (1957),p.298.

p.124 Bertrand Russell (1978),pp.303-304.

p.125 John Osborne (1957),pp.93-94.

Bibliography

Alexander, M. Wayne and Judd, Ben (1978) 'Do Nudes in Ads Enhance Brand Recall?', *Journal of Advertising Research*, Volume 18(1), pp.47–50.

Allen, Woody (1983) *Four Films of Woody Allen*, Faber and Faber; London.

Alvarez, A. (1971) *The Savage God*, Weidenfeld and Nicolson; London.

Ateyo, D. (1973) 'The Mating Game', *Time Out*, 14 December, pp.10–13.

Barash, David P. (1978) *Sociobiology and Behaviour*, Heinemann; London.

Barrett, William (1979) *The Illusion of Technique*, William Kimber; London.

Berger, Peter L., Brigitte Berger and Hansfried Kellner (1977) *The Homeless Mind*, Penguin: Harmondsworth.

Bieber, Irving (1964) 'Footnote', *Time*, p.213.

Brown, George and Tirril Harris (1978) *Social Origins of Depression*, Tavistock: London.

Bruner, Jerome S., Jaqueline J. Goodnow and George A. Austin (1956) *A Study of Thinking*, John Wiley: New York.

Burke, Charles (1977) *Loneliness*, St. Mary's College Press: Minnesota.

Cancian, Francesca M. (1987) *Love in America*, Cambridge University Press: Cambridge.

Chodorow, Nancy (1978) *The Reproduction of Motherhood*, University of California Press: Berkeley.

Clare, Anthony (1986) *Lovelaw*, BBC: London.

Clare, J. (1972) 'Marriage: cupid from the computer'. *The Times*, 26 March p.7.

Colman, Marshall (1982) *Continuous Excursions*, Pluto Press: London.

Danilov, A. (1972) 'Do You Want to Be Happy'. *Current Digest of the Soviet Press*, Vol.25 part 8, p.18.

Davidoff, Leonore (1973) *The Best Circles: Society Etiquette and the Season*, Croom Helm: London.

Didion, Joan (1979) *The White Album*, Simon and Schuster: New York.

Downing, John (1980) *The Media Machine*, Pluto Press: London.

Duck, Steve (1983) *Friends, For Life*, Harvester Press: Brighton.

Ehrenreich, Barbara, Elizabeth Hess and Gloria Jacobs (1987) *Re-Making Love: The Feminization of Sex*, Jonathan Cape: London.

Fischer, Claude S. and Susan L. Phillips (1982) 'Who is alone? Social characteristics of people with small networks', pp.21-39 in Letitia Anne Peplau and Daniel Perlman (eds) 1982 *Loneliness. A Sourcebook of Current Theory, Research and Practice*, Wiley – Interscience Publications: New York.

Fisher, Wesley A.(1980) *The Soviet Marriage Market: Mate Selection in Russia and the Soviet Union*, Praeger Publishers: New York.

Friedan, Betty (1965) *The Feminine Mystique*, Penguin: Harmondsworth.

Fromm, Erich (1975) *The Art of Loving*, George Allen and Unwin: London.

Fromm, Erich (1978) *To Have or To Be?*. Jonathan Cape: London.

Fromm-Reichmann, Frieda (1959) 'Loneliness', *Psychiatry*, Vol. 22 pp.1-15.

Gathorne-Hardy, Jonathan (1981) *Love, Sex, Marriage and Divorce*, Jonathan Cape: London.

Gerzon, Mark (1982) *A Choice of Heroes*, Houghton, Mifflin: Boston.

Gonick, Jean (1987) *Mostly True Confessions*, Grafton: London.

Goode, William J. (1959) 'The Theoretical Importance of Romantic

Love', *American Sociological Review*, Vol. 24, pp.38- 47.

Gordon, Suzanne (1976) *Lonely in America*, Simon and Schuster: New York.

Gosling, Ray (1980) *Personal Copy*, Faber and Faber. London.

Gross, Martin L. (1978) *The Psychological Society*, Random House: New York

Jenner, Heather (1979) *Marriages are Made on Earth*, David and Charles: London

Johnson, Robert A. (1983) *We*, Harper and Row: London.

Hall, Stuart *et al* (eds) (1980) *Culture, Media, Language*, Hutchinson: London.

Hancock, Barry W. (1986) *Loneliness, Symptoms and Social Causes*, University Press of America: Lanham Maryland.

Harrison, A.A. and L. Saeed (1977) 'Let's make a deal: An analysis of relations and stipulations in lonely Hearts advertisements'. *Journal of Personality and Social Psychology*, Vol. 35 (4), pp.257-264.

Hartog, Joseph, (1980) 'Introduction: The Anatomization' pp.1- 12 in J. Hartog, J. Ralph Audy and Y.A. Cohen (eds) (1980) *The Anatomy of Loneliness*, International Universities Press: New York.

Hendry, Joy (1985) 'Japan: Culture Versus Industrialization as Determinant of Marriage Patterns', pp.197-222 in Kinsley Davis (ed) (1985) *Contemporary Marriage. Comparative Perspectives on a Changing Institution.*

Henry, Jules (1980) 'Loneliness and Vulnerability' pp.95-110 in J. Hartog, J. Ralph Audy and Y.A. Cohen (eds) *The Anatomy of Loneliness*, International Universities Press: New York.

Himes, Norman E. (orig. 1936, 1970) *Medical History of Contraception*, Schocken: New York.

Hinde, Robert A. (1982) *Ethology*, Fontana: London.

Hochschild, Arlie Russell (1983) *The Managed Heart*, University of California Press: Berkeley.

Hodgkinson, Liz (1986) *Sex is Not Compulsory*, Columbus: London.

Jahoda, Gustave (1959) 'Love, Marriage, and Social Change: Letters to the Advice Column of a West African Newspaper', *Africa*, Vol. 29 pp.177-189.

Jen Huang, Lucy (1979) 'Notes on the Official View With Regard to Mate Selection and Marital Happiness in the People's Republic of

133

China', pp.218-226, in George Kurian (ed) (1979) *Cross-Cultural Perspectives of Mate Selection and Marriage*, Greenwood Press: Connecticut and London.

de Jong-Gierveld, Jenny and Jos Raad Schelders (1982) 'Types of Loneliness' pp.105-119 in Letitia Anne Peplau and Daniel Perlman (eds) (1982) *Loneliness. A Sourcebook of Current Theory, Research and Therapy*, Wiley – Interscience Publications: New York.

Joseph, Roger (1979) 'Sexual Dialectics and Strategy in Berber Marriage', pp.191-201 in George Kurian (ed) (1979) *Cross-Cultural Perspectives of Mate Selection and Marriage*, Greenwood Press: Connecticut and London.

Kiefer, Christine W. (1980) 'Loneliness and Japanese Social Structure', pp. 425-450 in J. Hartog, J. Ralph Audy and Y.A. Cohen (eds) (1980) *The Anatomy of Loneliness*, International Universities Press: New York.

Kundera, Milan (1984) *The Unbearable Lightness of Being*, Faber and Faber: London.

Kurtz, Irma (1983) *Loneliness*, Basil Blackwell, Oxford.

Larkin, Philip (1983) *Required Writing*, Faber and Faber: London.

Lasch, Christopher (1978) *The Culture of Narcissism*, W.W. Norton: New York.

Literaturnaya gazeta (1975) '"Get Aquainted!" What the First 500 Letters Told Us', in *Current Digest of the Soviet Press*, Vol. 28, No 52, p.12.

Little, Kenneth and Price, Anne (1969) 'Some trends in Modern Marriage Among West Africans, *Africa*, Vol. 37 pp.407-424.

Lobodzinska, Barbara (1979) 'Love as a Factor in Marital Decision Making in Comtemporary Poland', pp. 250-267 in George Kurian (ed) *Cross-Cultural Perspectives of Mate-Selection and Marriage*, Greenwood Press: Connecticut and London.

Lopata, Helena Z. (1973) 'Loneliness: Forms and Components', pp.103-115 in Robert Weiss (ed) (1973) *Loneliness: The Experience of Emotional and Social Isolation*, M.I.T. Press: Massachusetts.

Lynch, James J. (1977) *The Broken Heart. The Medical Consequences of Loneliness*, Basic Books Inc: New York.

Macfarlane, Alan (1986) *Marriage and Love in England. Modes of Reproduction 1300-1840*, Basil Blackwell: Oxford.

McGough, Roger (1987) *Melting into the Foreground*, Penguin: Harmondsworth.

Mailer, Norman (1957) *The Naked and the Dead*, Grafton; London.

Malinovsky, L. (1975) '"Friendship" Correspondence Club', *Current Digest of the Soviet Press*, Vol. 28, No 52 p.13.

Manuel, E. Frank and Fritzie P. Manuel (1979) *Utopian Thought in the Modern World*, Basil Blackwell: Oxford.

Maris, Ronald W. (1981) *Pathways to Suicide*, John Hopkins University: Baltimore.

May, Rollo (1975, orig. 1953) *Man's Search For Himself*, Souvenir Press Ltd: London.

Morgan, Robin (1980) *Take Back the Night*, Vintage Books: New York.

Moustakas, Clark E. (1961) *Loneliness*, Prentice-Hall, Englewood Cliffs: New Jersey.

Mullan, Bob (1983) *Life as Laughter: Following Bhagwan Shree Rajneesh*, Routledge ad Keegan Paul: London.

Mullan, Bob(1984) *The Mating Trade* Routledge and Keegan Paul: London.

Neville, Richard (1971) *Playpower*, Paladin: London.

Osborne, John (1957) *Look Back in Anger*, Faber and Faber: London.

Packard, Vance (1972) *A Nation of Strangers*, David McKay Company Inc: New York.

Parker, Dorothy (orig.1944, 1973) *The Penguin Dorothy Parker*, Penguin: Harmondsworth.

Peck, M. Scott (orig. 1978, 1987) *The Road Less Travelled*, Century: London.

Peplau, Anne and Daniel Perlman (1982) 'Theoretical Approaches to Loneliness' pp.123-134 in Letitia Anne Peplau and Daniel Perlman (eds) (1982) *Loneliness. A Sourcebook of Current Theory, Reserach and Therapy*. Wiley – Interscience Publications: New York.

Perevedentsev, V. (1977) 'Bachelor Cities', in *Current Digest of the Soviet Press*, Vol. 29 Part 7.

Polhemus, Ted (1978) *The Body Reader*, Pantheon: New York.

Prakasa, V.V. and Nandini Rao, V. (1979) 'Arranged Marriages: An Assessment of the Attitudes of College Students in India', pp.11-31 in George Kurian (ed) (1979) *Cross-Cultural Perspectives of Mate Selection and Marriage*, Greenwood Press: Connecticut and London.

Raj Gupta, Giri (1979) 'Love, Arranged Marriage and the Indian Social Structure', pp.168–179 in George Kurian (ed) (1979) *Cross-Cultural perspectives of Mate Selection and Marriage*, Greenwood Press: Connecticut and London.

Reich, Charles A. (1972) *The Greening of America*. Penguin: Harmondsworth.

Reisman, David (1969) '"The Lonely Crowd", 20 years After', *Encounter*, Vol. 33, Oct. 1969 pp.36–41.

Rogers, Carl (1973) *Carl Rogers on Encounter Groups*, Harper and Row: New York.

Root, Jane (1984) *Pictures of Women* Pandora: London.

Roszak, Theodore (1970) *The Making of the Counter Culture*, Faber and Faber: London.

Rubin, Zick (1970) 'Measurement of Romantic Love', *Journal of Personality and Social Psychology* Vol. 16, No 2 pp.265–273.

Russell, Bertrand (1978), *The Autobiography of Bertrand Russell*, Unwin Paperbacks: London.

Rusell, Daniel (1982) 'The Measurement of Loneliness' pp.81–104 in Letitia Peplau and Daniel Perlman (eds) *Loneliness. A Sourcebook of Current Theory, Research and Practice*, Wiley – Interscience Publications: New York.

Sadler, William A. and Johnson, Thomas B. (1980) 'From Loneliness to Anomie', pp.34–64 in J. Hartog, J. Ralph Audy and Y.A. Cohen (eds) (1980) *The Anatomy of Loneliness*, International University Press: New York.

Sarton, May (1986) *Journal of a Solitude*, Woman's Press: London.

Schlapentokh, Vladimir (1984) *Love, Marriage, and Friendship in the Soviet Union. Ideas and Practices*, Praeger Publishers: New York.

Schur, Edwin (1976) *The Awareness Trap*, McGraw-Hill: New York.

Seager, Joni and Ann Olson (1986) *Women in the World*, Pan: London.

Sennett, Richard (1977) *The Fall of Public Man*, Cambridge University Press: Cambridge.

Segalen, Martine (1986) *Historical Anthropology of the Family*, Cambridge University Press: Cambridge.

Stone, Alan A. (1985) 'Emotional Aspects of Comtemporary Relations. From Status to Contract', pp.397–414 in Kingsley Davis (ed) (1985) *Contemporary Marriage, Perspectives on a Changing Institution*, Russell Sage Foundation: New York.

Sullivan, Harry Stack (1953) *The Interpersonal Theory of Psychiatry*. Norton: New York.

Tillich, Paul (1980) 'Loneliness and Solitude', pp.547–553 in J. Hartog, J. Ralph Audy ad Y.A. Cohen (eds) (1980) *The Anatomy of Loneliness*, International Universities Press: New York.

Vaughan, Paul (1972) *The Pill on Trial*, Penguin: Harmondsworth.

Warhol, Andy and Pat Hackett (1981) *Popism: the Warhol '60's*, Hutchinson: London.

Weiss, Robert (1973) *Loneliness: The Experience of Emotional and Social Isolation*, MIT Press Cambridge: Massachsettes.

Weiss, Robert (1982) 'Issues in the Study of Loneliness' pp.71–80 in Letitia Anne Peplau and Daniel Perlman (eds) (1982) *Loneliness. A Sourcebook of Current Theory, Research and Therapy*, Wiley – Interscience Publication: New York.

Whitehead, Ted (1972) *Alpha Beta*, Faber and Faber: London.

Wilson, Amrit (1978) *Finding a Voice: Asian Women in Britain*, Virago Press: London.

Wilson, Edward O. (1978) 'Foreward', pp.xiii–xv in Barash (1978).

Wilson, Glenn and David Nias (1977) *Love's Mysteries*, Fontana: London.

Winship, Janice (1980) 'Sexuality for Sale', pp.218–223, in Hall *et al* eds, (1980).

Wolf, Margery (1986) 'Marriage, Family, and the State in Contemporary China', pp.223–251 in Kingsley David (ed) (1985) *Contemporary Marriage. Perspectives on a Changing Institution*, Russell Sage Foundation: New York.

Wolfe, Tom (1976) *The Painted Word*, Bantam: New York.

Yankelovich, Daniel (1981) *New Rules*, Random House: New York.

Zilboorg, G. (1938) 'Loneliness', *Atlantic Monthly*, January, pp.45–54.

Index